Robert Louis Stevenson's

TREASURE
ISLAND

A PLAY BY
Nicolas Billon

Coach House Books | Toronto

first edition

 Canada Council   Conseil des Arts
for the Arts   du Canada

 ONTARIO ARTS COUNCIL
CONSEIL DES ARTS DE L'ONTARIO
an Ontario government agency
un organisme du gouvernement de l'Ontario

Canadä

Published with the generous assistance of the Canada Council for the Arts
and the Ontario Arts Council. Coach House Books also acknowledges the
support of the Government of Canada through the Canada Book Fund and
the Government of Ontario through the Ontario Book Publishing Tax Credit.

LIBRARY AND ARCHIVES CANADA CATALOGUING IN PUBLICATION

Billon, Nicolas, author
    Treasure Island / Nicolas Billon.

Adaptation of: Treasure Island / Robert Louis Stevenson.
Issued in print and electronic formats.

ISBN 978-1-55245-350-6 (softcover).
    I. Title. II. Stevenson, Robert Louis, 1850-1894. Treasure Island

PS8603.I44T74 2017   C812'.6   C2017-900552-9
                                             C2017-900553-7

Treasure Island is available as an ebook: ISBN 978 1 77056 517 3 (EPUB),
ISBN 978 1 77056 518 0 (PDF), ISBN 978 1 77056 522 7 (MOBI).

Purchase of the print version of this book entitles you to a free digital copy. To
claim your ebook of this title, please email sales@chbooks.com with proof of
purchase. (Coach House Books reserves the right to terminate the free digital
download offer at any time.)

To my friend, Jon Kaplan.

Production History

Treasure Island was originally commissioned by the Stratford Festival, Ontario, Canada (Antoni Cimolino, Artistic Director and Anita Gaffney, Executive Director).

The play had its world premiere on June 3, 2017, at the Festival's Avon Theatre. The cast and crew were as follows.

Father, Long John Silver: Juan Chioran
James, Jim Hawkins: Thomas Mitchell Barnet
Mother, Dr. Livesey: Sarah Dodd
Bennett, Ben Gunn: Katelyn McCulloch
Captain Smollett: Jim Codrington
Squire Trelawney: Randy Hughson
Billy Bones, O'Brien: Bruce Hunter
George Merry: Ujarneq Fleischer
Pew, Arrow: Deidre Gillard-Rowlings
Black Dog: Gordon Patrick White
Israel Hands: Victor Ertmanis
Aunt Fanny, Roberta: Yolanda Bonnell
Allardyce: Jamie Mac
Tom Morgan: Nicholas Nahwegahbow
Abraham Gray: Jimmy Blais
Hunter, Joyce: Zlatomir Moldovanski
Ruth Less: Miali Buscemi
Ruth More: Tahirih Vejdani

Director: Mitchell Cushman
Set Designer: Douglas Paraschuk
Costume Designer: Charlotte Dean
Lighting Designer: Kevin Fraser
Composer & Sound Designer: Debashis Sinha
Projection Designer: Nick Bottomley
Fight Director: John Stead

Aeralist Coach: Katelyn McCulloch
Assistant Director: Tyler J. Seguin
Stage Manager: Maxwell T. Wilson
Assistant Stage Manager: Kim Lott
Assistant Stage Manager: Zeph Williams
Assistant Stage Manager: Brian Scott
Production Stage Managers: Anne Murphy, Julie Miles,
    Marylu Moyer

Dramatis Personae

The Pirates

Long John Silver, *ship's cook.*
Israel Hands, *coxswain.*
George Merry, *boatswain.*
Tom Morgan, *able-bodied sailor.*
Roberta, *able-bodied sailor.*
William O'Brien, *able-bodied sailor.*
Joyce, *able-bodied sailor.*
Allardyce, *unintelligible able-bodied sailor.*
Ruth Less, *able-bodied sailor and inseparable friend of –*
Ruth More, *able-bodied sailor.*
Red Shirt, *able-bodied sailor.*
Billy Bones, *curmudgeonly pirate.*
Black Dog, *curmudgeonly pirate.*
Pew, *blind and curmudgeonly pirate.*

The Not-Pirates

Jim Hawkins, *cabin boy.*
John Trelawney, *squire.*
Dr. Diana Livesey, *ship's surgeon.*
Alexander Smollett, *ship's captain.*
Ben Gunn, *marooned ex-pirate.*
Abraham Gray, *carpenter's mate.*
Hunter, *Trelawney's servant.*
Arrow, *first mate.*
Fanny, *Jim's aunt.*

Neither Pirate nor Not-Pirate

James, *sibling.*
Bennett, *sibling.*
Father, *their father.*
Mother, *their mother.*

Pre-Show

Lobby

Ushers greet audience members as they file into the theatre. Adults are given the play program. Kids, on the other hand, receive a rolled-up treasure map.

No doubt there will be a vexed adult or two who will ask for – nay, demand – a map for themselves. But ushers will be under strict orders: only kids are allowed to get one.

There are four hidden letters in the map: F, O, L, D.

On the back of the map is a strange, abstract pattern.

Theatre

Adults and kids find their seats. On stage is Billy Bones. He has a long, prominent scar along the right side of his cheek – a wound from some frightful fracas on the high seas?

Billy looks through a mounted spyglass. He searches the horizon for something … or someone …

Kids (and only kids) can join Billy onstage and take a peek through his spyglass. Billy shares with them what he's looking for: 'Pirates … especially a one-legged pirate. Can you help me find him?'

One by one, kids take a look through the spyglass. What they see is not the theatre, but a virtual-reality video of the breathtaking English cliffs near the Admiral Benbow Inn. Exactly what Billy Bones would see in Treasure Island.

The kids are primed for theatrical magic as the lights go down and the curtain rises …

Act 1

Scene 1

Lights up.

We're in the bedroom of siblings James and Bennett. They sleep in a bunk bed, with James on the bottom bunk.

Seated on a sea chest by the bed is Father. He reads from a dog-eared copy of Treasure Island.

James is enthralled. Bennett, aloof, plays a game on her phone and wears earbuds.

As Father reads, vignettes with the sights and sounds of a pirate battle materialize upstage as shadow puppetry.

FATHER: Billy Bones was a silent man by custom. All day he hung round the cove or upon the cliffs with a brass telescope; all evening he sat in a corner of the inn and drank rum and told stories. It were these stories what frightened people worst of all. Dreadful stories they were – about hanging, walking the plank, and storms at sea, and wild deeds on the Spanish Main. But the most ghastly stories were those involving the treasure of Captain Flint. Legend says Flint took six ashore to bury the treasure, but came back … alone!

JAMES: What happened to them?

FATHER: Nobody knows. The crew often wondered about it … Their dreams were haunted by it, haunted by the words of Captain Flint's favourite song …

JAMES: 'Dead Man's Chest!'

FATHER: *(sings)* Fifteen men on a dead man's chest –
Yo-ho-ho and a bottle of rum!
Drink and the devil had done for the rest –
Yo-ho-ho and a bottle of rum!

(*reads*) But Billy Bones held his peace that evening, and for many evenings to come. (*shuts book*) All right. Time for bed.

Father stands up and blows a good-night kiss to James.

JAMES: Good night, Dad.

FATHER: I'll see you soon. Good night, mateys!

JAMES: Yar!

Father exits.

BENNETT: (*removes her earbuds*) What?!

JAMES: Nothing. Just … good night.

BENNETT: Night. Weirdo.

The siblings prepare for sleep, then –

JAMES: I want to know what happens next!

BENNETT: You're going to snore and fart in your sleep.

JAMES: I mean in *Treasure Island*.

BENNETT: Never read it, so … I dunno. Treasure. On an island.

JAMES: Everyone's scared of Captain Flint because he's so badass.

BENNETT: If Captain Flint's so badass, it's 'cause *he* is probably a *she*.

JAMES: Girls can be pirates?!

BENNETT: Ugh. You're such a boy.

A crinkling noise echoes in the dark.

JAMES: What are you doing?

James gets out of bed and aims a flashlight at Bennett.

Bennett holds some individually wrapped cheese.

BENNETT: (*mouth full*) Cheese!

She hands one to James.

JAMES: I'm not hungry.

BENNETT: Save it for later. Dork.

James puts the cheese in the breast pocket of his pyjamas.

He stores the dog-eared copy of Treasure Island *inside the sea chest.*

JAMES: I think Billy Bones is hiding something in his sea chest. He's worried about pirates coming, so he must have something they want, right? Like ... Well, it can't be treasure, 'cause he carried the chest himself ... Maybe ... a map! He must have a map to the treasure!

A flutter of wings echoes through the air –

What was that? Bennett?

Another flutter of wings –

Did you hear that?

James shines the flashlight on the top bunk –

Bennett's bed is empty.

... Bennett?

Another flutter of wings –

Something swooshes over James's head.

James waves his flashlight to catch sight of it, and the beam of light falls on –

Scene 2

The snarling face of Billy Bones!

James yelps.

Lights shift as we move into the world of Treasure Island.

BILLY BONES: This 'ere the Benbow Inn?

JAMES: Uh ...

BILLY BONES: This is a handy cove, 'tis. Much company, mate?

James shakes his head.

Well, then, this is the berth fer me. I'm a plain man. Rum 'n' bacon 'n' eggs is wot I want.

This all sounds familiar to James ...

JAMES: You're Billy Bones, aren't you?

Billy Bones puts a hand on his cutlass, steps back –

BILLY BONES: Who wants to know?

JAMES: No one! I've just heard of you, that's all.

BILLY BONES: Aye, well, can I help if me exploits are known far and wide? But keep me name to yerself, lad. Ye might call me 'Captain' to be safe.

JAMES: All right.

BILLY BONES: Now, I've a favour to ask ye.

JAMES: Sure.

BILLY BONES: Keep yer weather eye open fer a seafaring man with one leg. If ye see 'im, come tell me straight away.

JAMES: I will.

BILLY BONES: Good lad.

Billy Bones grabs the sea chest –

JAMES: Hey …

BILLY BONES: And don't touch me sea chest!

He exits.

James turns and finds himself –

Scene 3

— at the bar of the Admiral Benbow Inn.

FANNY: (*offstage*) … and pay your bill, David Balfour!

Fanny barrels into the room, a bundle of clothing under one arm.

She stops when she sees James.

JAMES: Hello.

FANNY: (*re: pyjamas*) What are you wearing?

JAMES: What?

FANNY: You're not a parrot, Jim Hawkins.

JAMES: Jim Hawkins?

FANNY: Oh, you makin' fun of me now?

JAMES: No! I would never … (*lightbulbs*) I'm Jim Hawkins!

FANNY: If you're expectin' a reward for knowin' your own name, you'll be standing there a while yet. (*notices*) And why you goin' about in plain daylight with a candle?

James raises his hand – his flashlight has magically turned into a candle. He looks at it, mesmerized.

She throws him the clothes.

Get changed and get to work. The inn don't run itself, do it?

Fanny exits.

James dons a serving apron. He is now Jim Hawkins.

Jim finds a handkerchief in the apron pocket. He ties it around his neck as –

A suspicious-looking fellow with a suspicious-sounding name enters.

This is Black Dog.

He sits at a table and stares at Jim.

JIM: … Hello.

BLACK DOG: How 'bout some rum, then?

JIM: Oh, I don't drink.

Black Dog cocks his head.

You were asking for yourself. Of course.

Jim gets rum for Black Dog.

BLACK DOG: Tell me, lad. Is this 'ere table fer me mate Bill?

JIM: I don't know your mate Bill. But we have a guest who likes to be called the captain.

BLACK DOG: Well, me mate Bill would call 'imself the captain, as like as not. He has a mighty pleasant way with 'im, particularly in drink, has me mate Bill. We'll put it, fer argument like, that yer captain has a cut on one cheek – and we'll put it, if ye like, that the cheek's the right one.

JIM: That sounds like the captain.

BLACK DOG: Ah, well! Now, is me mate Bill in this 'ere house?

JIM: He's out for a walk.

BLACK DOG: Well, I'll keep me eye out fer –

Black Dog glances outside.

Talk of the devil! 'Ere he comes.

Black Dog hides, and motions Jim to his side.

Aye, let's give 'im a little surprise.

Jim joins Black Dog.

Billy Bones enters and heads for his table –

Black Dog steps out of hiding.

'Ello, Billy.

Billy Bones spins round.

BILLY BONES: Black Dog!

BLACK DOG: And who else? Black Dog as ever was, come fer to see his old shipmate. Ah, Billy. We have seen a sight of times, us two, since I lost them two talons.

Black Dog holds up his hand: he has two fingers missing.

BILLY BONES: Ye ran me down; here I am. Well, then: speak.

BLACK DOG: Yer in the right of it, Billy. I come to take back wot's rightly ours, is all.

BILLY BONES: Then ye've come a long ways fer naught.

BLACK DOG: Come now, Billy. Don't be like that. We can work –

Billy Bones draws his cutlass.

BILLY BONES: Ye always talk too much, Black Dog.

Black Dog pushes Jim toward Billy Bones.

Billy Bones spins Jim to safety behind him.

This gives Black Dog time to draw his own cutlass.

The two pirates engage in a spirited sword fight. Black Dog is stronger and more aggressive, but Billy Bones is smarter and more experienced.

Billy Bones narrowly misses a death blow; Black Dog swings again and catches Billy Bones on his right side.

Billy Bones goes down on one knee and furiously staves off Black Dog's thrusts.

And just when it looks like it's the end for Billy Bones –

Fanny enters. She aims a rifle at Black Dog.

FANNY: Whatever disagreements you may 'ave with my lodger will 'ave to wait. Best be on your way.

Unfazed, Black Dog glares at Fanny.

She cocks the rifle.

Black Dog chuckles. He steps away from Billy Bones and exits.

Fanny follows after him to make sure he doesn't lurk about.

Jim helps Billy Bones onto a chair.

BILLY BONES: Rum, Jim. I'll need some rum.

JIM: I'll go get Dr. Livesey –

BILLY BONES: Don't worry about that, lad. I needs to get away from 'ere, and a tipple o' rum will give me courage enough to keep going .

Billy Bones wobbles up to his feet –

And crumples to the floor.

JIM: Aunt Fanny!

The lights shift –

Scene 4

Billy Bones lies on the bed of his room at the Admiral Benbow.

He groans in pain. His sea chest lies at the foot of the bed.

Dr. Diana Livesey, the local doctor, examines the patient. The prognosis is not good.

Jim enters with a platter of food.

LIVESEY: Well, Mr. Billy Bones, if that be your name –

Jim sets the platter on the sea chest –

BILLY BONES: (*not himself*) Don't touch me sea chest!

Startled, Jim jumps back.

Billy Bones finds his bearings again.

BILLY BONES: Sorry, lad ... Sorry.

LIVESEY: Mr. Bones, you need to rest and give your wound time to heal.

BILLY BONES: I needs to get away from 'ere, doctor.

LIVESEY: You're bed-bound for at least a week, whether you like it or not.

BILLY BONES: But –

LIVESEY: It's for your own good. And no more rum – doctor's orders. Understood?

BILLY BONES: Aye, I'll stay off the stuff fer now. Upon my honour, I will.

Livesey gives Billy Bones a dubious look and exits.

JIM: Anything else you need, Captain?

BILLY BONES: Just one thing, lad. (*then*) Rum.

JIM: The doctor just said –

BILLY BONES: Doctors is all swabs! That doctor there, why, wot do she know about living on the high seas? I been places hot as pitch and mates dropping round with Yellow Jack, and I lived on rum, I tell ye. It's been man and wife to me.

JIM: I'm sorry. I can't.

BILLY BONES: Look, Jim, how my fingers fidges. I can't keep 'em still, not I. If I don't have a dram o' rum, Jim, I'll have the horrors; I seen 'em …

Billy Bones fishes out a key that hangs around his neck.

BILLY BONES: I'll give ye a golden guinea fer a noggin …

JIM: I don't want your money, Captain, but what you owe my aunt.

BILLY BONES: Please, lad. I beg ye.

JIM: I'll get you one glass, and not one more.

BILLY BONES: Aye, bless ye.

Jim turns to go –

Jim. Ye may be the last honest lad left in this world. I admire ye fer that, I do. Black Dog and the others, they is no better than a mischief of bilge rats. They don't deserve Flint's Fist. (*points to his sea chest*) Take it, Jim, if it ever comes to that, ye hear?

Jim nods and steps out into –

Scene 5

– the bar and fetches a glass of rum for Billy Bones.

A tap-tap-tapping fills the air. It gets closer and closer …

A woman with a green cloth over her eyes, Pew, enters. She's blind and guides herself with a stick.

PEW: Will any kind friend inform a poor blind woman, who has lost the precious sight of 'er eyes in the gracious defence of 'er native country, where or in what part of this great land she may now be?

JIM: You are at the Admiral Benbow Inn, Black Hill Cove.

PEW: Will ye give me yer hand, my kind young friend, and lead me to a table?

Jim goes to Pew, takes her hand –

Pew crushes Jim's hand with a vice-like grip. All kindness vanishes from her voice.

Now, boy, take me to the captain.

JIM: He's gone! He was in a fight and left right after –

PEW: And where did he go? What direction?

JIM: Uh …

BILLY BONES: (*offstage*) Jim! Rum!

PEW: I'd know that filthy voice anywhere.

Pew wrenches Jim's arm.

Jim yells out in pain.

Lie to me again, boy, and I'll snap yer arm like a twig! Now take me to 'im.

Jim has no choice but to lead Pew into –

Scene 6

– Billy Bones's room.

Jim brings Pew to the side of the bed.

JIM: He's in the bed in front of you.

Billy Bones floats in and out of consciousness.

Pew whacks him with her stick.

Billy Bones howls in pain. He sees Pew and recoils as if from a nightmare.

BILLY BONES: Pew!

PEW: Now, Bill, stay where ye are. If I can't see, I can hear a finger stirring. Business is business. Boy, take his left hand and bring it near to me right.

Jim does as he's told.

Pew puts a piece of paper in Billy Bones's left hand.

And now that's done.

Pew releases Jim's hand, turns, and strides out of the Admiral Benbow on her own – she's memorized the layout!

JIM: Captain –

BILLY BONES: Shh!

Billy Bones looks at the paper in his hand. He squints, tries to see what's written …

Jim, lad, I can't hardly see me own fingers. Wot's wrote here?

Jim takes the paper.

JIM: It's a black spot.

Billy Bones cringes and bites his hand.

JIM: That's ... not good, then?

BILLY BONES: The black spot! It's a summons, one ye don't come back from. I'm done fer, Jim.

JIM: There must be something we can do!

BILLY BONES: I'll ne'er give 'em wot they want, ye hear? (*then*) I'll do them yet, I will. There's still time to get away from here –

Billy Bones gets out of bed, invigorated with a sudden burst of energy and purpose.

JIM: What are you doing? The doctor said –

Billy Bones goes to his sea chest –

BILLY BONES: Never mind that, no, I just need to ...

He stops, suddenly, and puts a hand over his heart –

Jim!

Billy Bones crashes to the floor, struck dead by a heart attack.

JIM: Captain?

Fanny enters. She sees Billy Bones –

FANNY: Again?

JIM: (*checks vitals*) This time, he's dead. (*then*) We need to leave. The people who are after him ... They're coming back!

FANNY: And who'll pay for all this damage?! This'll ruin us.

Fanny's mention of money reminds Jim –

JIM: Hold on.

Jim takes the key from around Billy Bones's neck.

He goes to the sea chest, unlocks it –

Jim opens the sea chest and rummages through Billy Bones's belongings.

Aunt Fanny!

He throws her a money purse.

Fanny opens it and counts out her due.

FANNY: I'll show these rogues I'm an honest woman. I'll have my dues, and not a farthing over.

Jim unties his handkerchief and wipes his brow.

He continues to rummage through the sea chest and finds a rolled-up piece of cloth.

He unfurls it. It's a treasure map.

He rolls it up and takes it with him.

Fanny returns the purse to the sea chest.

Jim shuts it and they head out of the bedroom –

Scene 7

– into the Admiral Benbow bar.

They freeze as a mob outside the inn jeers and taunts Billy Bones.

Jim and Fanny are too late – the pirates are here!

Jim thinks fast and opens a secret compartment in the bar. He and Fanny hide there, just as –

Six pirates burst through the door. Armed with cutlasses, they all wear cloaks and black eye masks to conceal their identity. One pirate carries a huge maul.

Pew follows the others into the Admiral Benbow.

PEW: Find 'im! Find 'im, ye shirking lubbers! Find 'im and bring 'im 'ere!

From the bedroom, a familiar voice echoes out –

BLACK DOG: Bill's dead, Pew.

PEW: Did ye search 'im?

BLACK DOG: Aye.

PEW: And?

BLACK DOG: Nothing.

PEW: Is his sea chest there?

BLACK DOG: Aye.

PEW: Is it locked?

BLACK DOG: Aye.

PEW: Did ye find a key on Billy?

BLACK DOG: No.

PEW: Well, force it open, ye skulk!

BLACK DOG: Aye.

Black Dog rushes back into the bedroom. He grabs the maul, swings it back, and is about to smash the lock —

One of the pirates puts up her hand.

The pirate takes the lock off the chest — the shackle wasn't secured!

MASKED PIRATE (RUTH LESS): Idiots!

MASKED PIRATE (RUTH MORE): Yar, idiots!

They open the chest. The belongings are thrown about, pell-mell.

BLACK DOG: Pew, someone's turned the chest out alow and aloft. (*grabs money purse*) They left the money!

PEW: What about Flint's Fist?

Black Dog looks in the chest. Something catches his eye —

He pulls out Jim's handkerchief.

Black Dog runs over to Pew.

BLACK DOG: No. But I found that boy's kerchief in the sea chest!

Pew takes the handkerchief.

PEW: It's still damp. He can't have gone far! (*apoplectic*) Find him! I should've put his eyes out when I had the chance …

The pirates search for Jim. They get closer and closer to his hiding place —

A gunshot echoes in the distance.

BLACK DOG: Wot's that?

PEW: Keep searchin'!

A masked pirate runs in.

MASKED PIRATE (GEORGE MERRY): We'll have to budge, mates. Lawmen on horses comin' up the road!

PEW: Budge? Cowards! That boy's so close, I can smell him – and ye want to run? Shiver me soul, if I had eyes!

The pirates hesitate …

Another gunshot.

That seals it: the pirates disperse.

Dogs! How dare ye? (*realizes she's alone*) Ye won't leave old Pew, mates? Not old Pew!

Silence. Then more gunshots and the neighing of horses.

Livesey, accompanied by Squire Trelawney and Hunter, enter the Admiral Benbow Inn, their weapons drawn.

LIVESEY: Who's there?

PEW: I … I don't know what happened. A young lad was helping me when a band of ruffians stormed in … They ran away when they 'eard gunshots.

TRELAWNEY: Which way did they go, my good lady?

PEW: (*points*) That a'ways, I believe, kind sir.

Trelawney nods to Hunter and they head out.

LIVESEY: Where's the young boy who was helping you?

PEW: I'm not sure … He hid when he 'eard the brigands. He can't 'ave gone far.

Livesey crosses the room –

LIVESEY: Jim?

Pew hears Livesey turn away from her; she pulls a dagger from her cloak and prepares to throw it at Livesey –

Jim, from his hiding spot, sees this –

JIM: Doctor!

Livesey turns and steps aside as –

Pew's dagger whistles by her head!

She shoots Pew. The blind woman falls to the ground, dead.

Jim and Fanny come out of hiding.

Trelawney and Hunter run back in –

TRELAWNEY: What happened?

JIM: She was one of the pirates.

TRELAWNEY: Doesn't surprise me at all. There was something suspicious about her. I knew it right away.

LIVESEY: And the others?

TRELAWNEY: Scattered to the wind, I'm afraid.

HUNTER: I'll go check the back, squire.

Trelawney nods and Hunter goes out.

JIM: How did you know to come save us, Doctor?

LIVESEY: Hunter overheard two of those ruffians talking down at the pub about wringing Old Billy's neck over at the Benbow.

TRELAWNEY: Hunter warned us and we rushed to your aid.

JIM: I think I know what they were looking for.

Jim unfurls the map on a table.

I found this in the Billy Bones's sea chest.

TRELAWNEY: It's a map. (*then*) Of an island!

LIVESEY: An inspired observation, as always, squire. (*looks closer*) This isn't just any map, Jim. See these initials on the bottom?

JIM: J. F.

LIVESEY: Jane Flint. I daresay, this is Flint's Fist – the map to Captain Flint's legendary treasure.

TRELAWNEY: Ah yes. And this X here must indicate where she's buried the treasure!

LIVESEY: (*holds her tongue*) Indeed.

TRELAWNEY: Oh, this is exciting. Very exciting.

JIM: What will we do with it?

TRELAWNEY: Why, we go after the treasure ourselves! I'll head to Bristol first thing in the morning. I'll hire the fastest ship and crew her with the ablest sailors. Livesey, you shall be ship's surgeon, of course, and you, Jim, shall be our cabin boy. How does that sound?

Jim beams, delighted, and turns to Fanny.

JIM: Aunt Fanny?

FANNY: Jim Hawkins, if your father – may he rest in peace – could see you now … (*to Trelawney*) You'll – (*thinks better of it; to Livesey*) You'll look after him?

LIVESEY: I'll protect him as I would my own son.

FANNY: Well, I s'ppose that's that, then.

Jim hugs Fanny.

LIVESEY: Now, squire ...

TRELAWNEY: What is it?

LIVESEY: People will be curious about the nature of our trip. It is of the utmost importance that we keep our true destination a secret.

TRELAWNEY: Of course, yes, that goes without saying –

LIVESEY: I say it because there are times, squire, when your enthusiasm leads you to share things that perhaps you shouldn't.

TRELAWNEY: That you would think me so gauche, Dr. Livesey, wounds me. I give you my solemn word, from this moment onward, I shan't speak the words aloud about our purpose or destination to any living soul.

LIVESEY: Thank you.

Trelawney claps Livesey on the shoulder and heads out to find Hunter.

TRELAWNEY: (*yells*) Hunter, get ready! Tomorrow we travel to Bristol, hire a ship, and sail for Flint's treasure island!

Livesey and Jim share a look of dismay.

Scene 8

The Bristol docks bristle with activity as the Hispaniola's crew (Tom Morgan, Roberta, Allardyce, Ruth Less, Ruth More, Abraham Gray) runs about with cargo, ropes, etc. They all whistle the pleasant tune of a sailor song.

Arrow, the first mate, oversees the operation, seconded by the boatswain, George Merry.

Trelawney speaks with the coxswain, Israel Hands, and a man seated on a crate, his back to the audience. The squire laughs at something the seated man says.

As Allardyce passes by Arrow –

ARROW: What's that song you're all whistling?

Allardyce speaks with a very thick accent.

ALLARDYCE: Yar, wot lit? 'Tis deed yar dittle ye, yoop neet marinor che dit!

ARROW: … Of course. Thank you.

ALLARDYCE: Yar don menton yit, ment hap aye.

Allardyce continues on his way.

ARROW: Did you understand a word of that, Mr. Merry?

MERRY: Aye, sir. Clear as day.

Livesey and Jim arrive at the dock.

Jim is mesmerized by this new world.

Trelawney goes over to greet them.

TRELAWNEY: Welcome to Bristol, my dear friends. I'm glad you were able to make the journey so promptly: our ship's company is now complete!

LIVESEY: Oh? In your last letter, you lamented the hardship of finding a sea-worthy crew.

TRELAWNEY: True, but I'd not yet had the good fortune of meeting Mr. John Silver, our ship's cook. He knows every sailor in town worth their salt. (*turns*) Long John!

The man seated on the crate turns to look at Trelawney; this is Long John Silver (played by the same actor as Father). The squire waves him over.

Silver stands up with the help of a wooden crutch – he has only one leg!

JIM: (*whispers*) Doctor, squire – Billy Bones warned me about a seafaring man with one leg. It was the only pirate he was afraid of!

TRELAWNEY: (*chuckles*) My dear Jim, this man is the opposite of a pirate. A better man I've rarely met.

Silver joins them.

TRELAWNEY: Long John, let me introduce you to the ship's surgeon, Dr. Livesey, and our cabin boy, Jim Hawkins.

SILVER: Pleased to meet you both.

TRELAWNEY: I was about to recount for them the harrowing tale of how you lost your leg while serving in the Royal Navy.

SILVER: In the service of King George, aye.

TRELAWNEY: You're the right sort of man, Silver. We're lucky to have you.

SILVER: Thank you, sir. (*notices Jim sussing him out*) Jim, are you fond of birds?

JIM: Birds? I don't know. I suppose so.

SILVER: Then I want you to meet someone.

Silver takes a thin silver whistle that hangs around his neck and uses it to emit a pleasant, high-pitched sound.

A familiar flutter of wings echoes out as a parrot flies down from above and lands on a nearby ledge.

Jim is enchanted by the parrot. He pets her.

Now, this bird is nearly 200 years old, Mr. Hawkins. If anyone has seen more wickedness, it must be the devil himself.

CAP'N FLINT: Pieces of eight! Pieces of eight!

SILVER: She's taken a shine to you, lad, which is saying something; she's a crotchety old girl.

JIM: What's her name?

SILVER: Cap'n Flint.

JIM: After the pirate?

SILVER: Aye. All she squawks about is treasure. Just like a pirate, wouldn't you say?

Jim nods.

At the other end of the docks, a suspicious-looking sailor with a suspicious-sounding name enters carrying a sack.

Jim gasps when he sees –

JIM: Black Dog! Stop him!

Black Dog freezes. The other sailors stop, unsure what to do.

ARROW: Stop that man!

Gray and Morgan move in on Black Dog.

SILVER: Catch him, you freshwater swabs!

Everyone springs into action and a physical, choreographed escape takes place. Ad lib: 'Get him!', 'Over there!', etc.

Black Dog weaves and dodges past everyone.

It looks like he'll get away, too, but just as he slips past one last sailor —

Silver uses his crutch and trips Black Dog!

Black Dog sprawls to the ground. Allardyce and Merry pin him down.

Silver turns to Jim.

Who is this Black … Black what?

JIM: Black Dog. (*to Trelawney and Livesey*) He's one of the pirates who came after Billy Bones!

ARROW: Then he shall face justice. (*to Allardyce and Merry*) Take him to the magistrate's office, if you please.

Allardyce and Merry pull Black Dog to his feet and exit with him.

SILVER: Did any of you know that man?

Shrugs and head shakes all around.

Good. (*to Arrow*) With your permission, sir, I'll post a guard at the gangplank and make sure only crew members come aboard.

ARROW: Excellent idea, Mr. Silver. And thank you for your help in apprehending him.

Silver touches his cap.

Arrow turns to Trelawney.

No pirate's to step foot on your ship, sir, not on my watch.

TRELAWNEY: Thank you, Arrow.

Silver goes to speak with Israel Hands.

LIVESEY: Does this allay your misgivings about him, Jim?

JIM: He does seem like the right sort of fellow.

TRELAWNEY: Indeed!

LIVESEY: When do we board?

TRELAWNEY: Right away, if you please. We'll be weighing anchor shortly. My good friends, we sail for treasure!

The set transforms as the sailors burst into 'Whup Jamboree' –

Scene 9

– and we are now on the deck of the Hispaniola.

At a nod from Arrow, Merry takes out a pipe and whistles for the crew to ready for departure.

The anchor is brought up, the sails are unfurled, and the Hispaniola *launches toward its destination.*

A sharp, no-nonsense man approaches Trelawney, Livesey, and Jim – this is Captain Smollett, skipper of the Hispaniola.

SMOLLETT: Squire, may I have a word?

TRELAWNEY: I am always at your orders, Captain Smollett.

Smollett pulls Trelawney aside. Livesey and Jim follow.

All's well, I trust?

SMOLLETT: Well, sir, better speak plain, I believe, even at the risk of offence. I don't like this cruise and I don't like the crew.

TRELAWNEY: Perhaps, sir, you don't like the ship?

SMOLLETT: She seems a clever craft; more I can't say.

TRELAWNEY: Possibly, sir, you may not like your employer, either?

Livesey steps in.

LIVESEY: Stay a bit. Such questions will only produce ill feeling.
(*to Smollett*) You say you don't like this cruise. Now, why?

SMOLLETT: I was engaged on what we call sealed orders to sail this ship where you should bid me. So far so good. But now I find that every sailor here knows more than I do. I don't call that fair, now, do you?

LIVESEY: No, I don't.

SMOLLETT: Next, I learn we are going after treasure – hear it from my own hands, mind you.

Livesey and Jim both turn to Trelawney. He shrugs.

Now, treasure is ticklish work; I don't like treasure voyages on any account, and I don't like them, above all, when they are secret and when – (*stares long and hard at Trelawney*) when the secret has been told to the parrot.

TRELAWNEY: I've not said a word to *anyone's* parrot.

SMOLLETT: It's a way of speaking, squire. Blabbed, I mean. It seems everyone knows everything about this 'secret' expedition.

TRELAWNEY: (*scoffs*) Now, now, Captain. Surely that is an exaggeration. They know we sail for treasure, granted. But that is all.

SMOLLETT: That we are sailing for Flint's treasure.

TRELAWNEY: ... Yes.

SMOLLETT: That you have a map of this island.

TRELAWNEY: ... Perhaps.

SMOLLETT: That the map has a red cross that indicates the exact location of the treasure.

TRELAWNEY: Conjecture, no doubt!

SMOLLETT: (*hands Trelawney a piece of paper*) And that this here is the exact longitude and latitude of Treasure Island, as indicated by your map.

From Trelawney's expression, it's clear the coordinates are correct.

TRELAWNEY: (*to Livesey and Jim*) Was it one of you?

LIVESEY: We arrived in Bristol this morning.

SMOLLETT: It matters little at this point. I don't know who has this map, but I ask that it be kept secret, even from me. Now, as for the crew, I should have had the choosing of my own hands.

LIVESEY: Are they not sea-worthy?

SMOLLETT: They have experience, but discipline is lax and I've noticed small acts of insubordination.

TRELAWNEY: Perhaps, Captain, it's because they don't like you.

SMOLLETT: That's as they please, sir. They'll find I do my duty; I hope they do theirs.

LIVESEY: Your objections are duly noted, Captain.

SMOLLETT: You are determined, then, to go on this cruise?

TRELAWNEY: Like iron.

SMOLLETT: Then may I make one suggestion: shift the arms from fore to aft, so that our cabins stand between them and anyone wishing access.

TRELAWNEY: I'll do it, but I think the worse of you.

SMOLLETT: And that's as *you* please, sir.

Jim gives Captain Smollett a dirty look.

The fore deck will also need to be swabbed down, Mr. Hawkins. Don't let us keep you. (*to Trelawney and Livesey*) I'll have no favourites on my ship.

Smollett takes his leave.

LIVESEY: Contrary to all my notions, I believe you have managed to get two honest men on board with you: Silver, and that man.

TRELAWNEY: Silver, I'll grant you. That one? He's an intolerable humbug.

Jim nods in agreement.

LIVESEY: Well, we shall see.

Up by the ship's wheel, Smollett confers with Gray.

SMOLLETT: Mr. Gray, I pray you keep your ears and eyes open on this voyage.

GRAY: Aye, sir. They seem a competent lot, though.

SMOLLETT: Indeed, Mr. Gray. Indeed.

Scene 10

A projection traces the voyage from the city into the Bristol Channel and then onwards to the Atlantic.

The map fades away and is replaced by a night sky with some cloud cover.

The deck empties until only Silver remains.

Jim comes up on deck.

SILVER: Come away, Hawkins. Come and have a yarn with me. Nobody more welcome than yourself, lad.

Jim joins Silver. They share a moment of quiet awe as they look up at the stars.

JIM: On a clearer night, we might see the Milky Way.

SILVER: Aye. (*then*) Ye know how to find yer way using the stars?

Jim shakes his head.

It's a skill every sailor must have, Hawkins. (*points to a star*) The secret is to locate Polaris, the north star. It'll always guide you home.

JIM: How do you find it?

As Silver teaches Jim, the projection highlights Ursa Major and Polaris.

SILVER: (*points*) See those stars, there? There's the handle, and there's the plough ...

JIM: Yes. It looks like a saucepan.

SILVER: (*chuckles*) Aye, like a saucepan. Now, those last two stars, they're called pointer stars. If you draw a straight line up from them, five times the distance between them, you hit one particularly bright star –

JIM: Polaris?

SILVER: (*nods*) And Polaris always points due north. Steadfast and trustworthy. (*puts his hand on Jim's shoulder*) That we should all be so lucky, aye.

Silver shifts position. Jim steals a glance at Silver's leg.

You wondering how I lost it, then?

Jim shrugs, embarrassed.

You're too polite to ask, Jim, and I appreciate your discretion. But you needn't be so with Old John. We're mates now, aren't we?

Jim beams at this and nods.

Cannonball tore my leg to shreds during the battle of Puerto Cabello, serving in his Majesty's Royal Navy. Wasn't a cook then. Quartermaster, aye, and a fine one at that.

JIM: I reckon you'd've made a good captain, too.

SILVER: Do you now?

JIM: Everyone on the ship respects you.

SILVER: Well, I don't take your vote of confidence lightly, Jim Hawkins. You're as smart as paint, that's clear as day. Your father must be mighty proud of you.

Jim looks away.

Sorry if that's a sore point, lad. Shouldn't make no assumptions.

JIM: No, it's fine … My father took ill a little while back and passed away.

SILVER: Aye, that must've been hard on you.

JIM: I never got to hug him goodbye.

SILVER: (*nods, solemn*) I've two children myself. A lovely young lady and a lad just about your age, Jim. Though I don't get to see them as much as I'd like to, on account of my travels.

JIM: Yeah …

Jim and Silver smile at each other, moved at the similarity of their plights.

SILVER: (*stands*) Well, them potatoes won't peel themselves, will they?

JIM: Do you want a hand?

SILVER: Aye, Jim. Thank you.

As they get up –

Arrow and Israel Hands burst onto the deck, both three sheets to the wind.

ARROW: (*sings*)
… brained with a marlinspike,
And the cook's throat was
marked belike –

HANDS: (*sings*)
…brained with a marlinspike,
And the cook's throat was
marked belike –

Hands sees Silver and takes a theatrical bow.

Confused, Arrow does the same.

HANDS: Evenin', Cap'n Silver.

ARROW: (*re: Silver*) Cap'n? Captain Cook! Ha!

HANDS: (*sings*) It had been gripped by fingers ten –

ARROW: (*sings*) … gripped by fingers ten –

SILVER: Aye, mates, best you go back to your quarters. Get some rest, like.

ARROW: We're enjoying the sea air, thank you … Cap'n!

SILVER: You're both making fools of yourselves in front of young Hawkins here. Get back below deck.

ARROW: (*funniest joke ever*) Aye, aye, Cap'n!

Hands and Arrow turn back toward the crew deck –

ARROW AND HANDS: (*singing*) And there they lay, all good dead men
    Like break o' day in a boozing ken –

JIM: What shameful behaviour.

In a flash, Hands draws his knife and beelines for Jim –

HANDS: Ye gots words fer me, cabin boy?

Silver steps in front of Jim.

SILVER: Lay a finger on Hawkins and you'll answer to me, Israel Hands.

Hands stops cold.

Now get below and sleep it off.

Hands and Arrow stumble back down below deck.

SILVER: That's rum for you, Jim.

JIM: I thought the rum was locked up.

SILVER: Never been on a ship that doesn't have a secret store somewhere.

Silver looks up at the sky. Dark clouds loom on horizon.

Those clouds bear some fight in them, Jim. Sound the bell!

Jim sounds the bell as a far-off rumble rolls through –

Scene 11

Thunder, lightning.

The Hispaniola *crashes into a storm system as the ship enters the Caribbean Sea.*

The crew bursts onto the deck as Captain Smollett directs them from the poop deck.

The storm intensifies as the crew desperately works to keep things under control –

Waves crash on the deck.

Ropes snap.

Jim joins the fray and does everything he can to help.

Smollett struggles to be heard above the tumult of the storm.

He sees Morgan lose his balance on the shrouds and tumble backward –

Morgan hangs on by his foot!

Without a moment's hesitation, Smollett bolts up the webbing and saves Morgan's life.

Meanwhile, Arrow stumbles onto the deck – still drunk as a skunk – and can do no better than flail about the ship.

Out of nowhere, Israel Hands appears beside Arrow and pushes her overboard. Ah, the cur!

Meanwhile, Jim deals with a rope that suddenly snaps –

He loses his balance and is about to join Arrow overboard when –

Gray grabs Jim and saves him from certain death. Phew!

Together, Jim and Gray get the rope under control as –

Finally, the storm abates.

The exhausted crew members head to their bunks below deck.

Jim stumbles over to the apple barrel, reaches in, but the remaining apples are all at the bottom.

He climbs in –

Moments later, a gentle snore issues from the apple barrel.

Scene 12

On the projection, the ship drifts toward an island.

The map morphs into a striking dawn sky.

Silver, Roberta, Merry, Allardyce, Israel Hands, and Tom Morgan come up from below deck.

Morgan leans against the apple barrel and jolts its occupant awake. Jim pops his head up –

SILVER: Our mate Pew lost her eyesight in the same fight where I lost my leg.

– then ducks back down into the barrel.

Fearsome battle it was: a Spanish galleon bursting with gold.

MORGAN: Ye took on a galleon?

SILVER: Aye, Flint was fearless, she was. We lost a lot of good people that day, Tom. But we got them in the end, and that plunder made those of us still standing very rich.

Roberta, Allardyce, Hands, and Merry all grunt in agreement.

MORGAN: You were all part of Flint's crew, I reckon?

SILVER: Aye, you reckon right. Flint's fortune is on Treasure Island; she didn't spend her money, she was a saver, like. Legend goes she took six ashore to bury the treasure, but came back … alone! Now with Flint gone, it's only fair that it go to us, don't you think?

MORGAN: Aye.

SILVER: Aye. Could be a share for you, too, if you join with us.

MORGAN: I ain't no pirate, Silver.

SILVER: Watch your tongue there, Morgan. I know you don't mean no insult, but I do beg your pardon: we're not pirates, we are gentlemen of fortune.

MERRY: Aye, gentlemen –

ROBERTA: And gentle*women* –

MERRY: – gentlemen *and* -women of fortune.

ALLARDYCE: Thal, righal worekwar fer ghal rok yar.

MORGAN: Wot'll 'appen to the captain? The squire, the doctor?

SILVER: That's up to them. Why shed blood if there's no need?

MORGAN: But Arrow…?

HANDS: Arrow fell overboard.

SILVER: Tragic.

ALLARDYCE: Sabord boor, yar.

SILVER: It'll be their own choice. You have my affy-davy on that.

MORGAN: Good. I want me conscience clear on that account. I've no quarrel with 'em.

SILVER: 'Course not. You're as smart as paint, that's clear as day. I'm sure your father must be mighty proud of you.

Jim seethes at these familiar words.

MORGAN: There's me hand on it now.

Silver shakes Morgan's hand.

SILVER: And a brave lad you are, and smart too, and a finer figurehead for a gentleman of fortune I never clapped my eyes on.

MORGAN: So wot's the plan, then?

ROBERTA: Yar, good question, because if I have to sing that stupid 'Whup Jamboree' one more time, I will throw myself overboard.

Allardyce, Hands, and Merry vocalize their agreement.

SILVER: For the moment, nothing. Patience, mates. We strike once we have the treasure aboard. Then, and only then, do we take over the ship. We'll divvy everything up and go on our merry way.

The pirates chuckle.

Now, grab me an apple, will you?

Morgan goes to the apple barrel, about to discover Jim –

RUTH LESS: Land ho!

RUTH MORE: Yar, land ho!

The apple is forgotten; the pirates race to the front of the ship as the rest of the crew come up from below deck.

Jim slips out of the apple barrel and goes to Livesey.

The crew points out into the audience – Treasure Island!

Jim whispers in Livesey's ear. She turns and whispers into Captain Smollett's ear; he nods.

Smollett rings the ship's bell.

SMOLLETT: Gentlemen and ladies, this land we've sighted is the place we've been sailing for. I was able to tell Mr. Trelawney that every person on board had done their duty, alow and aloft, as I never ask to see it done better. We are going to the cabin to drink your health and luck, and you'll have grog served out for you to drink our health and luck. I think it handsome. And if you think as I do, you'll give a good sea cheer for the gentleman that does it.

The crew bursts into 'Hip-Hip-Hooray!'

SILVER: One more cheer for Cap'n Smollett!

A second round of 'Hip-Hip-Hooray!'

Smollett, Livesey, Trelawney, and Jim head to the cabin as the crew gathers for a serving of grog.

Silver is the first served. He leans on the side of the Hispaniola *and sings a haunting solo of 'All for Me Grog.'*

The crew listens as —

Scene 13

– in the captain's cabin, Jim relays (through pantomime) the information he overheard to Captain Smollett, Livesey, and Squire Trelawney.

Silver's song turns into a whisper. This cues the end of Jim's tale.

LIVESEY: Mutiny! I can hardly believe it.

TRELAWNEY: Now, Captain Smollett, you were right, and I was wrong. I own myself an ass, and I await your orders.

SMOLLETT: No more an ass than I, sir. The cook, their leader? Ingenious.

LIVESEY: Silver's a remarkable man.

SMOLLETT: We must go on. If I gave the word to go about, they would rise at once. We have the map – which buys us time. And there are faithful hands: I've sailed with Abraham Gray many times, and I know he would never betray his duty. I assume we can count on your man Hunter, Mr. Trelawney?

TRELAWNEY: Without the shadow of a doubt.

SMOLLETT: That's five of us, six with young Mr. Hawkins, against over a dozen bloodthirsty pirates.

TRELAWNEY: We'll need guile to overcome those odds.

LIVESEY: What if you offer the crew shore leave for the afternoon?

TRELAWNEY: Silver won't allow everyone to go ashore.

LIVESEY: No, but perhaps most of the crew will go. It'll even the odds for us to take back the ship.

SMOLLETT: Silver will be suspicious if none of us go with them.

TRELAWNEY: You're right.

JIM: I'll go.

LIVESEY: Out of the question!

TRELAWNEY: Jim, lad, we couldn't let you do that.

JIM: Whatever treachery is afoot, I do not believe Silver would harm me.

SMOLLETT: Mr. Hawkins, I appreciate your courage, but treasure makes people act in unpredictable ways.

JIM: I'm willing to take the risk. I'll run off as soon as we make landfall. Once they see the *Hispaniola* is lost, they'll turn themselves in. What other choice will they have?

Livesey, Smollett, and Trelawney look at each other and nod. The logic is sensible.

SMOLLETT: All right, Jim. But we'll send Hunter with you. He can defend you if it comes to that.

They all shake Jim's hand.

LIVESEY: I admire your courage, Jim. You make me proud.

TRELAWNEY: Hawkins, I put prodigious faith in you.

SMOLLETT: Good luck, young man. By this afternoon, God willing, the ship will be ours again.

We focus back to the deck, where the pirates have now joined Silver in song.

SILVER AND PIRATES: (*sing*) And it's all for me rum, me jolly, jolly rum
> All for the gold and for Silver
> Well we sail on the seas, and the treasure we will seize
> And no one on the ship will be the wiser
> And it's all for me rum, me jolly, jolly rum!

The crew applauds.

Silver stomps his crutch on the deck and begins a new, more terrifying song –

SILVER: (*sings*) Fifteen men on a dead man's chest –

The crew responds in kind – they stomp their feet and join in a boisterous, menacing rendition of 'Dead Man's Chest.'

PIRATES: (*sings*) Yo-ho-ho and a bottle of rum!
Drink and the devil had done for the rest –
Yo-ho-ho and a bottle of rum!

And before our eyes, the crew of the Hispaniola *transforms from able-bodied sailors into bloodthirsty pirates.*

Uniforms are ripped and torn to reveal the garb of gentlemen and gentlewomen of fortune hidden underneath.

On the sail appears an animated Jolly Roger.

The Hispaniola's bowsprit morphs from a mermaid into a ominous, threatening figure.

A terrified Jim looks out into the audience –

Blackout.

Act 2

Scene 14

Lights up.

The stage is now Treasure Island.

One of the audience balconies, meanwhile, stands in for the Hispaniola.

Two small puppet rowboats fly over the audience, going from the Hispaniola *to Treasure Island.*

Livesey, Trelawney, and Smollett stand in the balcony. Smollett follows the boats with a spyglass.

LIVESEY: Do you see him?

SMOLLETT: Hawkins is in the first boat.

TRELAWNEY: Ah, excellent. He and Hunter will land before the second boat and run off with ease.

SMOLLETT: Oh no …

LIVESEY: What is it?

SMOLLETT: Hunter's on the second boat.

TRELAWNEY: How is that possible? I told him –

SMOLLETT: Silver must have split them up. Nothing we can do now. Let's take care of the three pirates left on board.

Smollett and Livesey exit. Trelawney lingers.

TRELAWNEY: Godspeed, Hunter.

Scene 15

Jim runs into the thick jungle.

SILVER: (*offstage*) Jim! Jim! Come back!

Jim searches for somewhere to hide ...

Suddenly, something moves in the trees. What is it? Animal or human? Friend or foe?

Jim takes a step forward ...

It moves again!

JIM: ... Hello?

Suddenly, something tumbles out of the trees – it's Ben Gunn (played by the same actor as Bennett).

BEN GUNN: Hello.

JIM: Hello.

Ben Gunn pinches Jim.

Ow!

BEN GUNN: Did that hurt?

JIM: Of course it hurt – you pinched me!

BEN GUNN: You're real! It's not a dream!

JIM: You're supposed to pinch yourself to see if it's a dream.

BEN GUNN: You are?

JIM: Yes. Try it.

BEN GUNN: I don't want to.

JIM: Why not?

BEN GUNN: Because. It'll hurt.

JIM: Who are you?

BEN GUNN: I'm Ben Gunn. Who are you?

JIM: Jim Hawkins.

BEN GUNN: I don't know any Jim Hawkins.

JIM: *I'm* Jim Hawkins.

BEN GUNN: Oh. Hello. I'm Ben Gunn. I haven't spoken to anyone in … (*counts to eight on her fingers*) three years.

JIM: Were you shipwrecked?

BEN GUNN: Marooned! I've been living off pignuts and oysters and pignuts and goats and oysters. And goats.

JIM: Goats?

BEN GUNN: And pignuts. And oysters.

JIM: Yes.

BEN GUNN: I have an important question for you, Jim Hawkins.

JIM: All right.

BEN GUNN: Pay close attention.

JIM: I am.

BEN GUNN: You see, I've been eating only pignuts and oysters and goats.

JIM: I know.

BEN GUNN: But do you know what I really want?

JIM: No idea.

BEN GUNN: Cheese. I'd give anything for some cheese. (*falls to her knees*) Please, Jim Hawkins. Do you have any cheese? I'll give you my total whole entire fortune for a piece of cheese. Any cheese at all. (*then*) Except goat's cheese. I do not want goat's cheese.

JIM: I'm sorry, I don't have any cheese …

Ben Gunn bursts into tears.

Please! Stop crying … Shh …

Jim suddenly lightbulbs.

He pulls out the cheese Bennett gave him in the first scene.

JIM: I have cheese!

Ben Gunn stops crying –

A light, as if from the heavens, shines down on Jim's cheese.

BEN GUNN: Cheese!

Jim hands Ben Gunn the cheese.

Ben Gunn rips it open and nibbles off a piece.

BEN GUNN: Thank you, thank you, thank you.

JIM: Now maybe you could help me …

BEN GUNN: My total whole entire fortune is yours, Jim Hawkins.

JIM: Well, okay, but right now I need to get back to my ship.

BEN GUNN: You have a ship?!

JIM: Well … of course.

BEN GUNN: Could you take me with you?

JIM: Sure. But I need to get back to the ship first. Do you know how I might?

BEN GUNN: Yes. (*then*) With a boat.

JIM: I don't have a boat.

BEN GUNN: Oh. (*then*) I do.

JIM: You do?

BEN GUNN: A tiny boat, just big enough for me and you if we squish and squoosh and squash together.

JIM: Where is it?

BEN GUNN: (*points*) It's hidden near the Oath tree.

JIM: Oath tree?

BEN GUNN: The branches are as twisted as a pirate's sense of honour.

JIM: Great, let's –

Voices approach.

BEN GUNN: Hide!

Ben Gunn pulls Jim up into the trees as –

Morgan and Merry run into the jungle.

MORGAN: I think I saw him over this way …

MERRY: Cabin boy!

Morgan and Merry exit as Silver, Ruth Less, Ruth More, and Hunter enter.

Hunter's hands are tied behind his back.

SILVER: … he ran into the jungle, I reckoned something was afoot. Now, Hunter, we know you're loyal to Trelawney, though I can't think why. He's a big, bumbling land lubber …

The pirates laugh.

HUNTER: He has a good heart.

SILVER: I believe it. But you need to think about yourself now, Hunter. About what side you want to be on. We'd be happy to have you with us, is the truth.

Hunter looks out toward the Hispaniola.

Ah, yes, the *Hispaniola*. Trouble is, I've left my three best fighters on the ship. (*then*) So what do you say?

HUNTER: I'm your prisoner, and as such I'll put down arms and won't fight no more. But duty is duty, Silver, you know that much.

SILVER: (*claps him on the shoulder*) And I admire you for sticking to your principles, I do.

Ruth Less and Ruth More push Hunter along into the jungle. They nod to Silver on their way out.

Silver sighs. Not what he was hoping for.

HUNTER: (*offstage*) Argh!

Ruth Less and Ruth More return, each wiping a knife clean of blood.

RUTH LESS: It's done.

RUTH MORE: Yar, it's done.

SILVER: Gather the others.

RUTH LESS: (*shouts*) Yar!

RUTH MORE: (*shouts*) Yar, yar!

The pirates assemble when –

Scene 16

Boom!

A cannon shot echoes through the air and splashes in the water.

ROBERTA: Wot's going on?

Silver takes his spyglass and looks over at the Hispaniola.

The pirates hold their breath –

SILVER: Ah, the captain and squire are abandoning ship, mates!

The pirates cheer.

Boom!

Another cannon shot.

Silver aims his spyglass into the audience –

Ah, the scurvy dogs! They've taken the rations and weapons with them.

A puppet boat – with the tiny figures of Smollett, Trelawney, Livesey, and Gray – moves away from the Hispaniola.

On the balcony are Israel Hands, William O'Brien, and Red Shirt. They bicker as they operate the cannon and attempt to sink the rowboat.

SMOLLETT: (*offstage, mic'ed*) Row hard as you can, Mr. Gray!

GRAY: (*offstage mic'ed, out of breath*) Yes, sir.

LIVESEY: (*offstage, mic'ed*) Careful, everyone – incoming!

Boom!

Water splashes.

SMOLLETT: (*offstage, mic'ed*) That was close. Hold fast, everyone.

TRELAWNEY: (*offstage, mic'ed*) Are we there yet?

LIVESEY: (*offstage, mic'ed*) Pull yourself together! Squire, as you are the best shot, perhaps it would be more helpful if you took aim at the gunner?

TRELAWNEY: (*offstage, mic'ed*) Quite right.

Bang!

Red Shirt is hit and floats down into the audience below.

ROBERTA: They shot Red Shirt!

The pirates grumble, incensed, mixed in with exclamations of confusion (e.g., 'Who's Red Shirt?').

MERRY: Where they headed, Long John?

SILVER: Only one place they'd be safe – the stockade!

Ben Gunn and Jim pop up from behind some foliage.

BEN GUNN: I know these pirates, Jim Hawkins. They're the ones who left me here to eat only oysters and pignuts and –

JIM: You were part of Captain Flint's crew?!

BEN GUNN: What? No. (*then*) Maybe. (*then*) Yes. (*then*) It's a long story.

JIM: It doesn't matter now. We have to stop them from getting to the stockade before my friends. Can you help me?

BEN GUNN: Yes. You go ahead and warn your friends. (*indicates pirates*) I'll slow them down.

JIM: Thank you, Ben Gunn.

BEN GUNN: You're welcome, Jim Hawkins. If you need my help again, just walk north of the stockade. I'll hear you coming …

Jim takes off for the stockade.

Ben Gunn, meanwhile, sneaks up on the pirates from above.

George Merry brings up the rear. He walks backward to make sure no one's on their tail.

Ahead of him is Allardyce. Ben Gunn slinks down from above and smacks Allardyce on the head.

ALLARDYCE: Whar dutt?!

Allardyce turns around, furious. He thinks Merry smacked him.

With Allardyce and Merry both looking one way, Ben Gunn smacks Roberta, who is just ahead of Allardyce.

Roberta turns around, fuming.

Allardyce smacks Merry.

Yar! Yore scutt scurer fou, dorer ye munstross!

MERRY: Wot?

Roberta comes over –

ROBERTA: Ye like to smack people fer no reason, ye filthy cur?

She smacks Allardyce.

The other pirates join in and tangle in a ridiculous fray.

Silver breaks up the fight.

SILVER: Enough with your petty squabbles, mates. Have you all forgotten why we're here? Remember you might be standing on Flint's treasure right now!

Several pirates look down, lulled by the idea that fortune may lie (literally) beneath their feet.

Come on!

The pirates head off and arrive outside the stockade.

As they approach, a Union Jack runs up the flagpole –

Gunfire erupts from the loopholes –

We're too late – retreat!

The pirates withdraw. As they do, the stockade swivels so that we are now –

Scene 17

– inside the stockade, where Gray, Trelawney, Livesey, and Smollett cheer as the pirates flee.

LIVESEY: Well, that was close … A few minutes later and we'd be the ones running for cover.

SMOLLETT: Too close, I'd say. When can we expect the consort to come to our rescue, Mr. Trelawney?

TRELAWNEY: Ah, well … They were to follow if we were a month late in returning …

SMOLLETT: So no time soon.

TRELAWNEY: I'm afraid –

Boom!

A cannonball whistles above their heads and crashes into the jungle behind.

TRELAWNEY: What's this? The stockade can't be seen from the ship, how are they … ?

LIVESEY: *(points to the Union Jack)* The flag! Captain, they must be using it to aim at us. Gray, take it down –

SMOLLETT: Strike our colours? Never. Besides, they're wasting precious powder. Let them.

GRAY: Someone's coming over the palisade!

Everyone shoulders their rifles and aims at the palisade –

A familiar figure climbs over …

LIVESEY: It's Jim!

Livesey runs over and takes the lad into her arms.

I was so worried …

TRELAWNEY: We're glad to have you back, lad. Is Hunter with you?

JIM: He … uh … No. (*shakes his head*) I'm sorry.

TRELAWNEY: Ah. I see. Well.

Trelawney nods and moves further off to mourn his friend.

JIM: What happened on the ship?

SMOLLETT: We were outmatched, that's what. Silver must've smelt the trap. The pirates were ready for a fight. We're lucky we managed to escape with most of the weapons and rations.

JIM: Did you manage to salvage the cheese?

SMOLLETT: This isn't the time to be fastidious, Hawkins.

JIM: It's not for me, it's for Ben Gunn!

LIVESEY: Ben Gunn?

JIM: She's been marooned on the island for three years and –

MERRY: (*offstage*) Flag of truce!

The stockade swivels once more –

Scene 18

– to a side view of the stockade.

Merry waves a white handkerchief.

MERRY: Flag of truce!

SMOLLETT: Who goes? Stand, or we fire.

MERRY: Cap'n Silver, sir, to come and make terms.

SMOLLETT: *Cap'n* Silver? Don't know him. Who's he?

SILVER: Me, sir. These poor lads have chosen me cap'n, after your desertion, sir. We're willing to parlay and come to terms, and no bones about it. All I ask is your word, Cap'n Smollett, to let me in then out of the stockade safe and sound.

SMOLLETT: If there's any treachery, it'll be on your side, and the Lord help you.

SILVER: I know a gentleman, and that's enough for me.

Silver climbs into the stockade, with some difficulty –

Will any of you give me a hand?

Jim steps forward –

Smollett puts his hand on Jim's shoulder and stops him.

Finally, Silver manages to get into the stockade.

SMOLLETT: Well?

SILVER: Well, here it is. We want that treasure, and we'll have it – that's our point! You would just as soon save your lives, I reckon, and that's yours. I never meant you no harm, myself.

SMOLLETT: We know exactly what you meant to do.

Silver squints at Smollett: how much does he know?

SILVER: Well. Here it is. You give us the map and we'll offer you a choice. Either you come aboard along with us, and I'll give you my affy-davy to clap you somewhere safe ashore, or you can stay here and I'll give my affy-davy, as before, to speak to the first ship I sight, and send them here to pick you up.

SMOLLETT: Is that all?

SILVER: Aye.

SMOLLETT: Very good. Now you'll hear me. If you'll come up one by one, unarmed, I'll engage to clap you all in irons and take you home to a fair trial in England. If you won't, my name is Alexander Smollett, and I'll see you all to Davy Jones. Now bundle out of here, please, hand over hand, and double quick.

SILVER: That's that, then?

Smollett nods.

Silver shuffles up and over the palisade. He turns back just before he exits –

Before an hour's out, I'll stove in your old block house like a rum puncheon.

SMOLLETT: Good day, Mr. Silver.

Silver disappears into the jungle.

Lively, everyone. They won't wait long to attack us. Mr. Trelawney, Mr. Gray: please man the loopholes. Dr. Livesey and myself will be ready with cutlasses, and Jim will help load the muskets.

Everyone is scrambling into position when –

A loud roar erupts from the jungle –

Here they come!

Scene 19

The pirates attack!

They descend on the stockade with the full force of their numbers.

Trelawney and Gray fire from the loopholes –

The pirates climb over the palisade, and Gray takes out his cutlass.

The battle shifts to a melee.

George Merry sneaks up on Jim Hawkins, and just as he's about to strike the young man –

Gray steps in and saves Jim. Gray and Merry get into an intense duel.

Smollett, meanwhile, finds his sword-fighting equal in Joyce.

In a fierce exchange, Joyce manages to wound Smollett!

The captain continues the fight in spite of his injury, and eventually prevails against Joyce – the pirate falls under a wicked thrust from Smollett.

Gray, meanwhile, does not have the same luck: he falls under Merry's treacherous cutlass.

But it's clear the pirates won't prevail. They beat a hasty retreat back into the jungle.

TRELAWNEY: That's right, run, you curs!

Livesey helps a fallen pirate – but it's too late.

Trelawney turns to face a sombre group: Smollett lies propped up, wounded; Gray gasps, on the doorstep of death.

The bittersweet taste of victory hangs in the air as the stockade swivels –

Scene 20

– and Livesey goes to Smollett, but he waves her away.

SMOLLETT: I'm fine; look after Mr. Gray, if you will.

Livesey goes to Gray. There's little she can do for the poor man.

GRAY: Be I going, doctor?

LIVESEY: You're going home.

Gray nods, solemn.

Jim sits by Gray and takes his hand.

JIM: I owe you my life twice over, Mr. Gray. I'm sorry I could not do the same for you. Forgive me.

Gray smiles.

GRAY: Would that be respectful like, from me to you, young sir? Howsoever, so be it, amen!

JIM: Bless you.

A moment of silence, then –

GRAY: Oh, look –

And without another word, Gray dies.

Livesey closes the poor man's eyes, then tends to Smollett's wound.

SMOLLETT: All's well with him; no fear for a hand that's fallen in his duty.

LIVESEY: I hope you're right, Captain.

SMOLLETT: We should move soon. Silver won't try a frontal attack again.

TRELAWNEY: Will he lay down arms?

SMOLLETT: Certainly not. No: if I was him, I'd be finding a way to bring the *Hispaniola*'s cannon ashore and use it against us. (*then*) And now we've no way to retake the ship.

Jim lightbulbs when Smollett says this.

JIM: What happened to the boat you came over in?

SMOLLETT: Smashed to smithereens by a cannonball moments after we landed.

TRELAWNEY: So we can't use it, I'm afraid.

Livesey finishes bandaging Smollett. She takes her satchel and goes over to Jim.

LIVESEY: Jim, where can I find this Ben Gunn? If she's been marooned, she must know the island inside and out …

JIM: She told me to walk north from here if I wanted to find her.

LIVESEY: (*nods*) I went through our rations, and I found this …

Livesey pulls out a wheel of cheese from her satchel.

JIM: Cheese!

LIVESEY: I'll be back before you know it.

JIM: Be careful.

LIVESEY: I always am.

Livesey looks over the palisade, then climbs over and disappears into the jungle.

TRELAWNEY: I do admire her courage.

Trelawney and Smollett engage in a hushed conversation.

Jim gathers his things, grabs a pistol …

With one look back at Trelawney and Smollett, he sneaks off –

Scene 21

Jim is at the Oath tree. Its branches are twisted every which way. A round object leans against the trunk, in plain view.

Jim searches for Ben Gunn's boat … But so far, no luck.

A noise makes him jump. He turns and is face to face with –

JIM: Ben Gunn!

BEN GUNN: That's my name! (*suspicious*) Have we met before?

JIM: It's me, Jim Hawkins.

BEN GUNN: I don't know anyone by that name.

JIM: But –

BEN GUNN: (*shushes Jim with her finger*) Hold on.

She pinches Jim.

JIM: Ow!

BEN GUNN: Jim Hawkins! (*embraces him*) I've missed you.

JIM: Uh, yeah … You should go find Dr. Livesey. She's out looking for you.

BEN GUNN: A doctor? Why? I'm fine. I feel absolutely completely definitely fine. Nothing wrong with me. At all. Ever.

JIM: That's not –

BEN GUNN: Wait. What kind of doctor is she?

JIM: Uh … I'm not sure.

BEN GUNN: A podiatric audiologist?

JIM: No.

BEN GUNN: A pediatric geriatrician?

JIM: No.

BEN GUNN: A piratological hepatologist?

JIM: No, I don't think so.

BEN GUNN: Oh no. Is she … a … a … (*terrified*) *dentist?*

Ben Gunn covers her mouth with her hands.

JIM: No, nothing like that. She just wants to talk to you.

BEN GUNN: (*palpable relief*) Oh, she's one of *those* doctors.

JIM: She has cheese for you.

BEN GUNN: I'll go find her. Right away.

Ben Gunn turns to leave, stops, then turns back.

BEN GUNN: Wait a second. Why are you here?

JIM: … No reason.

BEN GUNN: That is a fibbly fib-fib. A lie.

JIM: If I tell you, swear that you won't breathe a word to anyone.

BEN GUNN: I swear.

JIM: On what?

BEN GUNN: On what what?

JIM: You can't just swear it, you have to swear on something.

Ben Gunn looks down.

BEN GUNN: I swear on my feet.

JIM: No. Swear on something important to you. Swear on … swear on cheese. If you break your promise, you can never eat cheese again.

BEN GUNN: (*solemn*) I swear on cheese, Jim Hawkins, that I won't say a word to anyone.

JIM: I'm looking for your boat.

BEN GUNN: You're leaving?

JIM: No, I just need to get to the *Hispaniola*. I'm going to board her and free her from the pirates.

BEN GUNN: By yourself?

JIM: I'll have the element of surprise.

BEN GUNN: It'll take you … (*counts to eight on her fingers*) three hours to paddle against the current on your own. I'll help you row out to the ship, then come back to find Dr. Cheese.

Ben Gunn takes the round, crazy-looking object leaning on the tree trunk.

JIM: What's that?

BEN GUNN: The boat!

Jim looks at it, unconvinced.

Come on!

Ben Gunn hops into the boat, followed by Jim, and they rush off into –

Scene 22

– the ocean. As they paddle, the cloud cover clears and a beautiful crescent moon and a bright, star-filled sky hangs above them.

Jim looks up and stops paddling. Ben Gunn notices, looks up as well.

They take a moment to soak in the beauty above them.

JIM: I love the stars.

BEN GUNN: Look at the moon! So beautiful, hanging in the sky … I wrote a poem about the moon. Do you want to hear it?

JIM: Uh …

BEN GUNN: The moon has a face like the clock in the hall;
She shines on thieves on the garden wall,
On streets and fields and harbour quays,
And birdies asleep in the forks of the trees.
The squalling cat and the squeaking mouse,
The howling dog by the door of the house,
The bat that lies in bed at noon,
All love to be out by the light of the moon.

JIM: Yeah, that's a beautiful po –

BEN GUNN: But all of the things that belong to the day
Cuddle to sleep to be out of her way;
And flowers and children close their eyes
Till up in the morning the sun shall arise.

JIM: Huh. You really do love the moon.

BEN GUNN: Of course. It's made of cheese.

Jim points to the Milky Way.

JIM: There's the Milky Way!

BEN GUNN: (*teary-eyed*) Why is the sky so delicious, Jim Hawkins?

The boat arrives in the shadow of the Hispaniola.

Jim grabs onto one of the ropes.

JIM: I got it from here. Go find Dr. Livesey!

BEN GUNN: I will. Great best good luck, Jim Hawkins!

Jim climbs aboard the Hispaniola –

Scene 23

– and slips onto the ship's deck.

Drunken shouts issue from below. Jim hides as –

Hands and O'Brien burst onto the deck, both drunk.

O'BRIEN: Ye cheated me, ye scurvy dog!

HANDS: Liar! Dirty, good-fer-nothin' swab –

O'BRIEN: Liar?!

HANDS: Ye 'eard me!

O'BRIEN: That's it.

O'Brien draws his cutlass as he staggers about.

Hands watches, unfazed.

O'Brien raises his cutlass and swings down –

Take that!

Hands doesn't move: O'Brien is three metres away from him.

HANDS: Ye can't hold yer liquor any better than yer tongue, O'Brien. What kind of Irishman are ye?

O'BRIEN: Those be yer last words, Israel Hands!

O'Brien moves in closer, raises his cutlass –

Hands pulls out a knife and lunges at O'Brien – but his aim is off.

Treachery!

The two men engage in a ridiculous, slow-motion fight. They struggle to keep their balance and land a hit.

O'Brien connects and cuts Hands's thigh, which forces the coxswain to favour his other leg.

Finally, and by sheer luck, Hands stabs O'Brien.

O'Brien falls and dies without so much as an oath.

Exhausted, Hands drops his knife, teeters over to the railing, and slumps down against it. He loses consciousness.

Jim comes out of hiding. He goes to O'Brien and throws the cutlass and Hands' knife overboard with a splash.

Jim then cuts the hawsers and strikes the Jolly Roger.

Hands slowly regains consciousness and sees Jim.

HANDS: What the ... ?!

JIM: Hello, Mr. Hands.

HANDS: Cabin boy?

JIM: You'll call me Captain Hawkins, if you please. The hawsers have been cut, and I mean to get the ship into the North Inlet and beach her quietly there.

HANDS: (*chuckles*) I'd like to see ye do that, I would.

Jim heads for the ship's wheel –

HANDS: Wait, Cap'n Hawkins. I'll help ye if ye'll give me rum and dressing fer me wounds. Ye have me word.

JIM: I don't know if your word means much, Mr. Hands.

HANDS: I'm unarmed and wounded, and I've no desire to visit Davy Jones's locker yet.

JIM: You can have the bandages now, and your rum once the ship's moored.

HANDS: Ye know how to make a man sing, Cap'n Hawkins.

Jim grabs a shred of canvas and throws it to Hands.

The coxswain dresses his thigh.

Jim goes to the ship's wheel and steers the Hispaniola *into the North Inlet.*

This voyage is displayed on the projected map.

JIM: I see the North Inlet ahead, Mr. Hands.

HANDS: Steady, lad. Let's beach 'er gently. Starboard a little … so … steady … starboard … larboard a little … steady … steady … Now, me hearty – luff!

The Hispaniola *creaks as Jim steers her onto a sand bank.*

Aye, Cap'n Hawkins, she's beached steady now.

JIM: Thank you for your help, Mr. Hands.

HANDS: That rum will be thanks enough, Cap'n. Ye'll find it below deck.

Jim nods and heads below deck.

As soon as Jim disappears, Hands pulls out a small knife from a secret sheath and hides it behind his back.

Jim returns and hands the rum bottle to Hands.

Much obliged, Cap'n. Yer a man of yer word. (*points*) Be sure the mainsail is fastened.

Jim turns to check the rigging.

Hands grabs the knife and takes a step toward the young man –

Jim turns around and pulls out his pistol.

JIM: I did suspect some treachery, Mr. Hands. I'd hoped you'd learned your lesson.

HANDS: Well, now, Jim, seems we is at a stalemate …

JIM: I'd hardly call it that.

HANDS: Aye, yer right.

Hands steps forward.

JIM: Not another step.

HANDS: I beg to differ.

Hands takes another step. Jim pulls the trigger –

Nothing happens.

I can see the pistol's wet from here. Priming's no good, is't?

Jim runs up to the poop deck.

Hands pursues, slowed by his thigh injury.

At the stairs, Hands puts the knife in his mouth and pulls himself up one step at a time …

Jim reloads the gun … Hands gets closer and closer …

Jim finishes reloading as Hands stands up on the poop deck.

JIM: (*points pistol at Hands*) Stop right there. We know that I'll shoot, so best you give yourself up, Mr. Hands.

Hands deflates, faced with defeat.

HANDS: Aye, Cap'n –

In a blazingly swift move, Hands throws the knife –

It hits Jim in the shoulder .

At the same time, Jim shoots and hits Hands square in the chest.

The coxswain tumbles backward, over the railing, and splashes into the ocean.

Jim grabs a few shreds of canvas and the bottle of rum he brought up from below, then rushes over to the shrouds and clambers down the ship.

As Jim makes his way to the shore, the set swivels to become the stockade (lateral) and jungle.

Scene 24

Jim sits on the edge of the stage.

He braces himself to pull out Hands's knife from his shoulder and gives himself courage by imagining how he'll break the good news to the others.

JIM: That's right, Captain Smollett, I took back the ship.

He grits his teeth and pulls out the knife —

Argh!

He pulls down his shirt and reveals the bloody wound on his shoulder.

Jim takes the rum and grimaces as he pours the alcohol on his shoulder.

Why yes, squire, I fought Israel Hands all by myself.

Jim takes the canvas and wraps it around his shoulder to make a bandage.

It's just a scratch, Dr. Livesey. The important thing is that the *Hispaniola* is ours again.

He pulls his shirt back over his shoulder and gets up.

The jungle looms around him, dark and menacing.

(heads in one direction) The stockade is that way – (*stops, turns in another direction*) No, that way … (*stops, turns in opposite direction*) Or … ?

Uh-oh. Jim alone in the jungle, lost.

A creepy sound startles him.

Ben Gunn, is that you?

It isn't.

Despondent, Jim looks up at the sky —

And sees the stars.

The north star. It'll always guide me home.

Jim points to the sky and traces the handle then the plough, as Silver taught him, and lands on Polaris.

There it is …

With a reference point, Jim works out the direction of the stockade.

(looks up and smiles) Steadfast and trustworthy.

Jim heads off toward the stockade.

Scene 25

Dawn peeks over the horizon as Jim arrives outside the stockade.

JIM: (*whispers*) Doctor! Captain! It's Jim.

A loud snore echoes from inside the stockade.

(*whispers*) Squire, is that you?

Jim climbs over the palisade and into the stockade.

He bumps a sleeping body with his foot —

(*whispers*) Hello?

And then —

CAP'N FLINT: Pieces of eight! Pieces of eight!

Jim freezes in terror as the parrot wakes the sleepers —

Scene 26

In a flash, Jim is surrounded by pirates: Silver, George Merry, Roberta, Tom Morgan, and Allardyce.

They've taken over the stockade!

SILVER: So, here's Jim Hawkins, shiver me timbers! Dropped in, like, eh? Well, come, I take that friendly.

Still in shock, Jim says nothing.

Well, you must be asking yourself some questions right about now, I reckon.

JIM: I declare I have a right to know what's what, and why you're here, and where my friends are.

MERRY: Wot's wot, is it? Lad, ye got some nerve –

Silver puts up a hand to shush George Merry.

SILVER: Aye, fair's fair. See, Dr. Livesey came with a flag of truce. She negotiated a peace and we bargained and here we are. As for your friends, they've tramped; I don't know where they've gone.

JIM: That's it?

SILVER: That's it. Though they were quite angry with your desertion, lad. Dr. Livesey said she never wanted to see your ungrateful face again. That's a bit harsh, in my opinion. (*smiles*) As I reckon, the short and the long of it is here: you can't go back to your own lot, for they won't have you; and unless you start a third ship's company all by yourself, you'll have to join with Cap'n Silver.

JIM: Just like that, is it?

SILVER: None of us won't hurry you, lad. Take your bearings. Time goes so pleasant in your company, you see.

JIM: I've seen too much to believe a word you say, Silver. But there's a thing or two I'd like to tell you: your whole plan's gone to wreck, and if you want to know who did it – it was me! I was in the apple barrel the night we sighted land, and I heard your plan for mutiny and informed the captain before the hour was out.

ROBERTA: Curse ye, boy! Yer why we is eating pignuts fer breakfast, lunch, and dinner!

The pirates grumble their disgust at the mention of pignuts.

RUTH LESS: I hate pignuts!

RUTH MORE: Yar, I – actually, I don't mind them.

JIM: You'll curse me again this morning, because I've just come back from the *Hispaniola*. I cut her cables and left her adrift …

Morgan runs out of the stockade and looks out toward the ocean.

MORGAN: She's gone!

JIM: Kill me, if you please, or spare me. But one thing I'll say, and no more. If you spare me, bygones are bygones, and when you're all in court for piracy, I'll save you best I can.

SILVER: (*amused*) I'll bear it in mind, Hawkins.

MERRY: I don't need no time to think about it, Silver. This 'ere lad's caused us enough trouble …

Merry draws his cutlass and steps toward Jim –

Silver wields his crutch to disarm Merry.

SILVER: Avast, there! Maybe you thought you was cap'n here?

A tense standoff between Silver and Merry.

ROBERTA: Aye, George's right, Silver. No point keepin' another mouth to feed, even if it's just pignuts –

RUTH LESS: I hate pignuts!

Ruth More can't respond: she's eating pignuts.

SILVER: Well, I like that boy. He's more courage than any pair of rats of you in this here house.

The pirates are somewhat befuddled by Silver's attitude.

They huddle into a corner and whisper amongst themselves.

You seem to have a lot to say. Pipe up and let me hear it.

MERRY: Ask yer pardon, sir. This crew 'as rights like other crews. I claim me right to a council.

Merry salutes Silver and moves to the far corner. The others join him after each one salutes Silver in the same manner.

SILVER: Now look you here, Jim. We're within half a plank of death. With the ship gone, they're going to throw us off. Now, you mark, I'll do everything I can to save your life. I says to myself, you stand by Hawkins, John, and Hawkins'll stand by you. You must promise to save me from swinging, Jim.

JIM: What I can do, that I'll do.

SILVER: It's a bargain, then. (*smiles*) Understand me, Jim. I've a head on my shoulders, I have. I'm on squire's side now.

The council of pirates returns to face Silver and Jim.

There's a breeze coming, Jim.

Morgan hesitates, then takes a step forward. He holds a piece of paper in his hand.

Hand it over, lubber. I know the rules, I do; I won't hurt a deputation.

Morgan hands the paper to Silver.

(*looks at the paper*) Ah, the black spot, is it? I thought so. Where did you get the paper – (*turns the paper over*) Look here, this ain't lucky! You've gone and cut this out of a bible. What fool's cut a bible?

ALLARDYCE: (*to Morgan*) Yar fore cuset fer al ernite!

MORGAN: (*to Merry*) See? Wot did I say? I tell ye it was bad luck, didn't I?

SILVER: Was it you had the bible, Tom? I'd get to prayers right away.

MERRY: Belay that talk, John Silver. This crew's tipped ye the black spot in full council. See wot's wrote there, then ye can talk.

SILVER: 'Deposed,' is it?

MERRY: Aye.

SILVER: You'll be cap'n next, I wonder.

MERRY: Someone's to make sure Hawkins gets wot he deserves.

SILVER: You fancy yourself a cap'n, George Merry, but you can't see further than your own nose. You got a plan then, do you, to get us out of this here predicament? I'd like to hear it.

The pirate all look at George Merry.

MERRY: I 'ave no plan this moment but to teach the young swab a lesson.

SILVER: That ain't a plan, that's your fool temper talking. That boy, why, are we going to waste a hostage? He might be our last chance, and I shouldn't wonder.

MERRY: Wot's a hostage good fer on this island?

SILVER: You a doctor, then, George Merry? Aye, you ain't, but this boy can get us the services of one. The doctor, she's fond of the lad and will help us in exchange for us treating him well. Did that ever cross your thick skull?

The pirates murmur in agreement – a valid point.

Besides, we just got to wait for the consort to show up in a few months, don't we?

ROBERTA: Months, like? And all we got to eat is …

Roberta stops, can't say the word.

RUTH LESS: I *hate* pig –

PIRATES: We know!

MERRY: Wait fer the consort to come and 'ang us, is wot they'll do.

SILVER: Unless we've got something to trade with, aye. You don't give me credit for thinking ahead, is what's wrong with all of you.

Silver puts his hand in his coat and pulls out –

Flint's map!

He throws it on the ground.

I bargained for the map as part of our agreement, you see. Which means today, you lubbers, we're going treasure hunting.

The pirates look at the map, stunned.

Merry kneels to pick it up, but Silver stabs the map with his crutch –

How do you feel about your cap'n now?

The pirates cheer. The mutiny is over – for now.

Silver takes his crutch off the map.

LIVESEY: *(offstage)* Hallo!

Livesey steps out of the jungle and holds a white handkerchief in her hands.

Silver looks out over the palisade.

SILVER: Good morning, Doctor.

LIVESEY: Silver! I – do you know the ship is gone?

SILVER: Aye, so it is. And we know who let it loose.

Silver nods for Jim to join him at the palisade.

LIVESEY: Jim!

SILVER: Came to say hello to us, which was very kind of him, don't you think?

LIVESEY: I'd like to speak with him, if I may.

SILVER: Give me a moment, then.

Silver hops down and takes Jim with him.

MORGAN: Ye won't let 'im, will ye?

SILVER: I don't see the harm in it.

MERRY: He'll slip away, sure as anythin'.

SILVER: Hawkins, will you give me your word of honour as a young gentleman not to slip your cable?

JIM: On my word of honour, John Silver.

SILVER: Aye, and he'll keep his word, I'm sure of that.

Silver and Jim return to the palisade.

All right, doctor. We'll give you a few minutes with the lad.

Jim and Silver make their way over the palisade.

(*to Livesey, sotto voce*) The boy'll tell you how I saved him. You'll please bear in mind it's not my life only now – it's that boy's into the bargain.

Silver sits against the palisade.

Livesey and Jim walk a few paces away –

Scene 27

– to the edge of the jungle.

Livesey pulls Jim into a hug.

LIVESEY: I thought I'd lost you.

Jim grimaces: the hug hurts his shoulder.

She notices his bandage.

What happened?

JIM: Nothing.

She pulls his shirt down; the canvas is bloody –

LIVESEY: Jim…

JIM: I'll be fine. I disinfected it with alcohol.

LIVESEY: You did?

Jim nods.

Livesey tucks a stray hair behind Jim's ear and smiles.

JIM: Silver told me you never wanted to see me again.

LIVESEY: What? No, I was just worried about you… (*glances at Silver*) Though I can't fathom your reasons for leaving us the way you did.

JIM: I'm sorry, but I knew if I told anyone what I was planning…

LIVESEY: I hope it was worth it.

JIM: I have the ship.

LIVESEY: What?!

JIM: She lies in the North Inlet, on the southern beach. Just below high water.

LIVESEY: Jim, I … I don't know what to say. Every step, it's you that saves our lives. You found out the plot; you found Ben Gunn – the best deed ever you did, or will do, by the way.

JIM: Why did you leave the stockade?

LIVESEY: We worried Silver was going to bring the cannon ashore, so we traded a few things we didn't need anymore for safe passage.

JIM: The map too?

LIVESEY: Jim, things are going to go poorly for these pirates very soon. Here, run away with me right now: we've got a good head start, and I have a pistol to cover our escape.

JIM: Doctor, I gave my word.

LIVESEY: I know. We can't help that now. I'll take the blame on my shoulders; but I cannot let you stay here.

Jim glances back at Silver.

JIM: No. I'm sorry, but I must keep my word.

LIVESEY: Please, Jim, I can't leave you here with them –

JIM: Doctor, I can't and I won't. My word of honour means something.

LIVESEY: Don't imagine we'll leave without you, young man.

JIM: Thank you.

Livesey kisses Jim on the forehead.

Jim returns to the stockade.

LIVESEY: Silver! A piece of advice.

SILVER: Aye?

LIVESEY: Don't be in a great hurry after that treasure.

And on that cryptic note, Livesey exits into the jungle.

SILVER: Now what do you think she meant by that, Jim?

Jim shrugs.

The pirates join Jim and Silver outside the palisade. They bear shovels, pick axes, and other accoutrements one might expect on a treasure hunt.

MERRY: We is ready, Long John! Time to get wot's ours.

SILVER: Eastwards!

The pirates cheer and sing 'Dead Man's Chest' as they journey to Flint's treasure, which leads them into –

Scene 28

– the audience.

The pirates trudge through the aisles and ad lib about the amazing and diverse wildlife (i.e., audience members) found on the island.

Twice, Silver abruptly change directions. It will soon become clear that, despite the map, he is lost.

MERRY: So. Which way now?

SILVER: Uh …

ROBERTA: Are we lost?

SILVER: (*struggles with the map*) No, no, we're not lost.

JIM: Maybe we could ask someone for directions.

The pirates gasp at Jim's audacity.

Silver speaks to Jim in a tone we've not heard him yet use.

SILVER: Now listen to me, Hawkins. If there's one thing a pirate'll never do, it's ask for directions.

The pirates all grunt in agreement … except for Roberta.

ROBERTA: (*to an audience member*) Well, *some* pirates ask fer directions.

JIM: Okay … What about asking for help?

The pirates murmur amongst themselves, intrigued by this idea.

SILVER: (*ponders*) I suppose it would be all right to ask for help. But no one can help us, because we're the only ones with a map.

Merry points to a kid with a map.

MERRY: This young whippersnapper's got a map!

ROBERTA: (*in a different spot*) This one too!

ALLARDYCE: (*in a different spot*) Yar, flergh ling gart urn took!

MORGAN: (*to Silver*) Ye said there was only one copy of the map!

JIM: Maybe there's a clue hidden in the maps?

The pirates work with the kids in the audience to find the hidden letters in the map, and yell out each one as they are discovered. When the four letters have been discovered …

SILVER: *O, F, D, L.* What does it mean, lubbers?

RUTH LESS: Dolf!

RUTH MORE: Flod!

RUTH LESS: Nar, Dolf!

RUTH MORE: Nar, Flod!

By this point, kids will (hopefully) be screaming, 'Fold!'

SILVER: Fold! Aye, mates, seems we've got to fold the map …

Together with the audience, the pirates fold the map in such a way that the back – the abstract pattern – transforms into the image of a tree with a skeleton on its trunk and, in the background, Spyglass Hill.

Aha! There it is, that's the landmark we've got to find.

MERRY: It's a big island, Long John.

SILVER: Aye, Merry. That's true. But perhaps this might be a good time …

Silver takes out his thin silver whistle from around his neck and blows into it.

Cap'n Flint flies over their heads as Silver shows him the map.

We need to get … here.

CAP'N FLINT: Pieces of eight! Pieces of eight!

SILVER: Exactly.

Cap'n Flint flies in the direction of the stage.

JIM: How does she do that?

SILVER: Cap'n Flint's got a special gift, Jim: Guiding Parrot Syndrome. GPS fer short.

The pirates make their way back to the stage –

Scene 29

— and arrive at a clearing, where a skeleton in tattered clothing hangs on a tree trunk.

Merry touches the clothes on the skeleton.

MERRY: That's good sea cloth, it is.

ROBERTA: Aye, that's a seaman.

SILVER: Aye, you wouldn't look to find a bishop here. Now, I reckon it should be a clue to point us the right way. But how?

The pirates examine the skeleton, desperate to figure out how it indicates the treasure.

CAP'N FLINT: Pieces of eight! Pieces of eight!

The arm on the skeleton shakes.

RUTH LESS: Did ye see that?

RUTH MORE: Yar, did ye see that?

The pirates look at the arm —

CAP'N FLINT: Pieces of eight! Pieces of eight!

The arm shakes again.

SILVER: That's it! We need to tell it what we're looking for. All together now, mateys.

PIRATES: Pieces of eight! Pieces of eight!

The arm shakes and rises a quarter of the way up.

MORGAN: Must be hard of hearing, Long John.
SILVER: Aye, we're gonna need some help.

Silver looks at the audience.

If only we had a crowd of loud, vivacious young lasses and lads who could help us on the count of three. If you help me, I give you my affy-davy to share the treasure with all of you. One ... two ... three ...

Silver ad libs as required to get the audience to shout, 'Pieces of eight!'

PIRATES AND AUDIENCE: Pieces of eight! Pieces of eight!

The skeleton's arm rises and points toward Spyglass Hill.

SILVER: Spyglass Hill! There's our line for the jolly dollars. But, by thunder! If it don't make me cold inside to think of Flint. This is one of her jokes, and no mistake. Her and these six was alone here; she killed them, every one, and this one she hauled here and laid down by compass, shiver me timbers! They're long bones, and the hair's been yellow ...

RUTH LESS: Thompson!

RUTH MORE: Yar, Thompson!

MERRY: Aye, that's right. I recognize his necklace.

ROBERTA: (*to Allardyce*) Thompson and ye were friends like, weren't ye?

ALLARDYCE: Tess bark scallywag me bucko ferk ash, yar.

Allardyce gently removes the skull and goes down on one knee. He is suddenly earnest and articulate.

Alas, poor Thompson! I knew him, a fellow of infinite jest, of most excellent fancy. He hath borne me on his back a thousand times, and now, how abhorred in my imagination it is! My gorge rises at it. Here hung those lips that I have kissed I know not how oft. Where be your gibes now? Your gambols? Your songs? Your flashes of merriment that were wont to set the table on a roar? Not one now to mock your own grinning? Quite chapfallen?

The pirates cough to get Allardyce's attention.

MERRY: Let's go, mate. We 'ave treasure to find.

ALLARDYCE: Yar, o' absely yute lurig harth, abse coure.

Allardyce leaves the skull and joins the other pirates.

JIM: (*to Silver*) What was that?

SILVER: (*to Jim*) Don't worry, just a bout of thespianitis. It comes over him now and then.

JIM: Is it contagious?

SILVER: Aye. Don't ever catch it, lad. It's a terrible affliction. (*points to Spyglass Hill*) Onward!

The pirates sing 'Dead Man's Chest' as they trudge forward —

Scene 30

– and arrive at Spyglass Hill.

As they pass by some thick foliage, Ben Gunn pops up. She holds a large conch in her hands. She puts it to her lips and disappears once again –

BEN GUNN: (*deep voice, sings*) Fifteen men on a dead man's chest – Yo-ho-ho and a bottle of rum!

The pirates all freeze in terror.

Ruth More jumps into the arms of Ruth Less.

MERRY: That … that sounded like Flint, didn't it?

ROBERTA: Do 'er ghost haunt the island?

SILVER: No, surely it's just some silly skylark …

BEN GUNN: (*deep voice*) Darby M'Graw! Fetch aft the rum, Darby!

MERRY: That were Flint's last words!

ROBERTA: Nobody in this 'ere island ever 'eard of Darby.

BEN GUNN: (*deep voice*) This is Captain Flint, and I tell you to turn back!

MORGAN: That fixes it! Let's go.

The pirates turn on their heels –

Silver doesn't move.

Belay there, John! Don't ye cross a spirit.

SILVER: Spirit? Well, maybe. But there's one thing not clear to me. There was an echo. Now, no man ever seen a spirit with a shadow; well then, what's she doing with an echo to her, I should like to know?

The pirates pause.

ROBERTA: Ye 'ave a 'ead upon yer shoulders, John, and no mistake. Echo ain't fer the spirit world.

BEN GUNN: (*deep voice*) Turn back! Turn back!

MERRY: And come to think on it, it was like Flint's voice, I grant ye, but not so clear-away like it. It was liker somebody else's voice now – it was liker ...

SILVER: (*lightbulbs*) Ben Gunn!

ROBERTA: Aye, and so it were. Ben Gunn it were!

The pirates draw their weapons.

SILVER: Come out and show yourself, Ben Gunn!

BEN GUNN: (*deep voice*) This is Captain Flint, and I tell you to turn back before I curse ye all!

Silver puts his finger to his lips and points to a patch of foliage.

SILVER: If you're Captain Flint, what is your middle name?

BEN GUNN: (*works it out*) Captain Jane Flint. My middle name is Jane?

The pirates pounce on Ben Gunn and pull her from the foliage.

SILVER: Well, well ... Look who it is.

BEN GUNN: You're not allowed to talk.

SILVER: I'm not, eh?

BEN GUNN: No. Only the person who holds the conch can speak.

The pirates look at Ben Gunn with confused expressions.

Silver takes the conch from Ben Gunn.

SILVER: You've got the wrong story, mate.

MERRY: On with it! The treasure's near.

SILVER: Aye, let's go.

Merry keeps a pistol trained on Ben Gunn as the pirates continue onward.

They arrive at the top of Spyglass Hill. There's a large sand pile with a big red X on it.

Morgan hands a shovel to Jim.

MORGAN: Here, cabin boy. Ye can get us started.

JIM: What?

MERRY: Aye, don't be lazy, Hawkins.

ROBERTA: And if I knows Captain Flint, she is sure to've buried it ten feet deep.

Jim plants the shovel in the sand –

Thunk.

He immediately hits pay dirt.

ROBERTA: Of course, she might 'ave been in a hurry …

The pirates (except for Silver) push past Jim and brush the sand away. It reveals a chest –

SILVER: Bring it here, mates!

The pirates move the chest over to Silver.

MORGAN: It's 'eavy!

MERRY: Aye, that there's the weight of wealth, Morgan!

Morgan and Roberta fumble with the lock.

With their attention elsewhere, Ben Gunn pulls Jim away from the others.

Merry prepares to use the pickaxe on the lock –

Ruth Less puts up her hand.

She takes the lock off the chest – the shackle wasn't secured!

RUTH LESS: Idiots!

RUTH MORE: Yar, idiots!

The pirates make a circle around Ruth Less as she lifts the lid of the chest –

Silence.

Ruth Less digs her hand into the chest. There's none of the satisfying metallic clink of coins –

Ruth Less cries. Is it joy? Is it fatigue? Is it …

RUTH LESS: Pignuts …

Pignuts go flying in every direction as the pirates dig through in search of treasure …

Nothing. The pirates turn to Silver.

RUTH LESS: Nothin' but pignuts …

PIRATES: We hate pignuts!

MERRY: Wot do ye 'ave to say, Silver? All this fer a chest full o' pignuts?

SILVER: Keep digging, you may find a guinea or two yet.

MERRY: Mates, do ye hear that? I tell ye now, that man there knew all along. Look in the face of him and ye'll see it wrote there.

SILVER: Ah, Merry, standing for cap'n again? You're a pushing lad, to be sure.

The pirates all draw their cutlasses.

MERRY: Aye, enough jest, Silver. This time, we're to have the last –

Three gunshots erupt from the jungle.

Merry, Morgan, and Roberta fall to the ground, dead.

Ruth More and Ruth Less escape into the jungle.

Allardyce stands, clearly waiting for a fourth bullet. None comes.

ALLARDYCE: Berg goot, ark fer tood, yar!

He celebrates by eating a pignut, and promptly chokes on it. He falls, dead.

Livesey, Squire Trelawney, and Captain Smollett emerge from the nearby foliage.

TRELAWNEY: In the nick of time, I say!

Jim rushes over and buries himself in Livesey's arms.

JIM: I thought we were done for!

LIVESEY: It took us some time to gather our weapons and make our way over. That's why we sent Ben Gunn ahead to try and slow them down.

SMOLLETT: When Dr. Livesey told us you'd managed to get our ship back, I was speechless.

JIM: I steered her into the North Inlet.

TRELAWNEY: Tremendous, quite simply tremendous. With the ship, we can sail back to Bristol.

SILVER: You're full of surprises, Jim Hawkins.

Jim smiles. He looks at the chest full of pignuts.

JIM: I'm only sorry there's no treasure after all …

TRELAWNEY: Tut, tut! I'm afraid that's not entirely true.

Jim looks at Trelawney and Livesey.

LIVESEY: We'll let Ben Gunn explain that one.

Ben Gunn entreats Jim to follow her.

Scene 31

Ben Gunn leads the group to her home in the jungle.

BEN GUNN: I found it … (*counts to eight on her fingers*) two years ago. I knew someone would come back for it.

JIM: So you brought it here …

Ben Gunn climbs up until she reaches a rope.

She pulls the rope, and a huge sheet filled with gold coins lowers from the canopy!

Jim and Silver gaze at the loot in complete awe.

Whoa …

SILVER: I can't believe it …

Ben Gunn nods, appreciative.

BEN GUNN: I promised you my total whole entire fortune, Jim Hawkins. Here it is! (*then*) And I know exactly what you're thinking. (*then*) 'How much cheese can I buy with all this?'

LIVESEY: I daresay, you'll have as much cheese as you'll ever want, Ben Gunn.

BEN GUNN: Really?

Everyone nods.

Ben Gunn bursts into tears.

Silver reaches for a coin. Trelawney smacks his hand.

TRELAWNEY: Gold's not for you, Silver.

SMOLLETT: We'll get the ship ready; Jim, you'll stay here and keep an eye on Mr. Silver. Make sure he doesn't fill his pockets.

SILVER: I'm a gentleman of fortune, Cap'n Smollett, not a thief.

SMOLLETT: Uh-huh.

Smollett, Trelawney, Livesey, and Ben Gunn exit.

JIM: I promise to do everything in my power to help you once we're in Bristol, Long John.

SILVER: I'm afraid I won't be going back with you.

JIM: Why not?

SILVER: I'm not one for the gallows. So I'll be making my own way, lad. (*then*) It was a true pleasure to spend time in your company, Mr. Hawkins.

JIM: I can't just let you go.

SILVER: Aye, lad, you must.

Silver moves toward the audience –

JIM: What about the treasure?

Silver stops.

SILVER: What about it?

JIM: I'll give you my share if you come with us.

SILVER: That's a mighty generous offer.

JIM: I mean it.

SILVER: I know you do. (*smiles*) Could I ask you for one coin?

JIM: One?

SILVER: Aye. Just one.

Jim picks up a coin and brings it to Silver.

SILVER: To pay for my passage.

JIM: I don't understand …

SILVER: It's time.

Silver pulls the thin silver whistle over his head and puts it around Jim's neck.

He tousles Jim's hair, then walks down into the audience.

JIM: I never got to hug you goodbye.

Silver turns back to Jim.

SILVER: I know. I wish we had. I'm sorry. (*then*) You have a good and kind soul. You're everything I wished for. (*then*) You'll always lead me home, son.

Silver turns back to the audience. He takes the coin, puts it in his mouth, then walks up the aisle as Jim watches him go.

Ben Gunn returns.

BEN GUNN: Where's Long John?

JIM: He's gone.

Ben Gunn joins Jim and sees Silver walking away.

BEN GUNN: Goodbye, Long John!

Silver turns around, sees Ben Gunn, and takes off his cap in salutation.

Ben Gunn waves goodbye.

Silver exits the theatre.

MOTHER: (*offstage*) James.

JIM: Did you hear that?

BEN GUNN: Yes.

Ben Gunn rushes off.

MOTHER: (*offstage*) James.

Jim tiptoes toward the sound –

Ben Gunn's cave recedes into darkness –

(*offstage*) James darling …

Jim makes his way back into –

Scene 32

— James and Bennett's bedroom.

Jim approaches the bed. He removes his Jim Hawkins clothes, back now to the same pyjamas he wore at the beginning.

Jim Hawkins is now James again.

Bennett is asleep on the top bunk.

James gets into his bed, under the covers, and —

Morning light floods the room.

A figure stands in the doorway, backlit.

MOTHER: Good morning, sleepyhead.

James sits up. The figure takes a step forward —

It's Mother (played by the same actor as Livesey). She wears hospital scrubs.

JAMES: Mom?

MOTHER: Hi, pumpkin. Just checking in. Aunt Fanny told me you were talking in your sleep.

James shrugs.

Bad dream?

JAMES: Sort of.

MOTHER: You want to tell me about it?

JAMES: Not right now.

MOTHER: Okay.

JAMES: How was the night shift?

MOTHER: Rough. (*then*) Waffles for breakfast?

JAMES: Yeah?

MOTHER: If you're okay sharing with Bennett.

JAMES: I guess.

Mother smiles and turns to leave –

Mom. (*then*) I miss Dad.

MOTHER: I know. Me too. (*puts her hand on his chest*) He'll always be in your heart, you know that?

James nods.

Mother kisses him on the forehead and exits.

James tousles his hair and yawns.

Suddenly, he feels something –

Jim pulls out the thin silver whistle from around his neck.

He blows into it; the whistle emits the same pleasant sound it did in his dream.

Nothing.

He whistles again.

Nothing.

James sighs and turns to head out after his mother –

A flutter of wings stops him –

Cap'n Flint flies over James's head.

CAP'N FLINT: Pieces of eight! Pieces of eight!

James looks up and a smile spreads across his face –

Blackout.

Curtain Call

After the actors have taken their bows, Jim steps forward and stops the music.

JIM: Before you all go … I think we should ask Long John to keep his promise to you.

SILVER: My promise?

JIM: You gave your affy-davy that if these young gentlemen and gentle-women of fortune helped you, you'd share the treasure with them.

Silver looks at the treasure …

Several of the pirates shake their heads: Don't do it!

SILVER: I don't remember making such a … (*to pirates*) Do any of you remember me saying such a thing?

The pirates ad lib variations of 'He never said that.'

JIM: (*to audience*) Do you remember Long John making that promise?

The audience will (hopefully) respond in the affirmative.

SILVER: (*clears his throat*) Well, it is possible…

Merry steps forward.

MERRY: Wot I 'eard him say wasn't 'share the treasure' but, uh …

ROBERTA: That he would, uh, swear …

MORGAN: That's right, swear … off …

RUTH LESS: Leisure!

RUTH MORE: Yar, leisure!

The pirates cheer, 'Swear off leisure!'

MERRY: So … No more fun fer you, Long John.

The pirates turn to head offstage –

SILVER: Avast there, mateys.

The pirates grumble to a stop.

Young Hawkins is right. I gave my affy-davy.

MERRY: Boo!

None of the other pirates follow suit. Merry hushes.

SILVER: (*to audience*) All right, lubbers. You helped me find the treasure, so you deserve your share of the loot!

Music and a festive atmosphere returns as the actors share the treasure (chocolate coins) with the audience.

'Dead Man's Chest'

In *Treasure Island*, Stevenson provides the chorus to a fictional ballad the pirates sing throughout the story. Numerous songs were created after the novel's publication based on Stevenson's chorus. For this adaptation, I chose a ballad called 'Derelict,' written by Young E. Allison in 1891. I made a number of modifications to suit my needs.

Fifteen men on a dead man's chest –
Yo-ho-ho and a bottle of rum!
Drink and the devil had done for the rest –
Yo-ho-ho and a bottle of rum!

The mate was fixed by the bosun's pike
The bosun brained with a marlinspike
And the cook's throat was marked belike
It had been gripped by fingers ten;
And there they lay, all good dead men
Like break o'day in a boozing ken –

Yo-ho-ho and a bottle of rum!

Fifteen men of 'em stiff and stark,
Ten of the crew had the murder mark!

There was chest on chest full of Spanish gold
With a ton of plate in the middle hold
And the cabins riot of loot untold,
And they lay there that had took the plum
With sightless glare and their lips struck dumb
While we shared all by the rule of thumb –

Yo-ho-ho and a bottle of rum!

Fifteen men of a whole ship's list
Dead and be damned and the rest gone whist!

We wrapped 'em all in a mains'l tight
With twice ten turns of a hawser's bight
And we heaved 'em over and out of sight,
With a 'Yo-Heave-Ho!' and 'Fare-you-well!'
And a sudden plunge in the sullen swell
Ten fathoms deep on the road to Hell –

Yo-ho-ho and a bottle of rum!

'Whup Jamboree'

A traditional sea shanty found by composer Deb Sinha. The lyrics include a few minor modifications.

Whup Jamboree, whup jamboree
Oh, a long-tailed sailor man comin' up behind
Whup Jamboree, whup jamboree
Come an' get your oats, me son

The pilot she looked out ahead
The hands on the cane and the heavin' of the lead
And the old man roared to wake the dead
Come and get your oats, me son

Whup Jamboree, whup jamboree
Oh a long-tailed sailor man comin' up behind
Whup Jamboree, whup jamboree
Come an' get your oats, me son

Oh, now we see the lizzard light
Soon, me dogs, we'll heave in sight
We'll soon be abreast of the Isle of Wight
Come and get your oats, me son

Whup Jamboree, whup jamboree
Oh a long-tailed sailor man comin' up behind
Whup Jamboree, whup jamboree
Come an' get your oats me, son

Trim the sails and for treasure we'll roam
Trim the sails and for treasure we'll roam

Now when we get to the black wall dock
Our legs will buckle when on land we walk
To the pubs and parlours all the sea dogs flock
Come and get your oats, me son

Whup Jamboree, whup jamboree
Oh a long-tailed sailor man comin' up behind
Whup Jamboree, whup jamboree
Come an' get your oats, me son

Well, then we'll walk down limelight way
And all our beaus will spend our pay
We'll not see more till another day
Come and get your oats, me son

Whup Jamboree, whup jamboree
Oh a long-tailed sailor man comin' up behind
Whup Jamboree, whup jamboree
Come an' get your oats, me son

Whup Jamboree, whup jamboree
Oh a long-tailed sailor man comin' up behind
Whup Jamboree, whup jamboree
Come an' get your oats, me son

(Concurrent Chorus)
Trim the sails and for treasure we'll roam
Sailing out on the ocean wide
Weigh the anchor, say goodbye to our home
We're sailing out under the golden sky

'All For Me Grog'

An old sea song, with once again a few modifications to the lyrics by
Deb Sinha.

I'm sick in the head and I haven't gone to bed
Since I first came ashore from me slumber
For I spent all me dough on the me lovers don't you know
Far across the western ocean I must wander

And it's all for me grog, me jolly, jolly grog
Gone is me gold and me silver
Well I spent all me tin on me lovers drinking gin
Across the western ocean I must wander
Across the western ocean I must wander

And it's all for me rum, me jolly, jolly rum
All for the gold and for Silver
Well we sail on the seas, and the treasure we will seize
And no one on the ship will be the wiser

And it's all for me rum, me jolly, jolly rum

Playwright's Acknowledgements

I would like to thank the following people and institutions for their help and support in bringing this adaptation of *Treasure Island* to life.

To the Stratford Festival and Bob White, Director of New Plays, for giving the go-ahead for this adaptation. My agent, Ian Arnold, made it work.

The delightful cast and creative team (listed at the front) behind *Treasure Island*'s first production in Stratford. Their contributions are peppered throughout the play.

The supportive and all-around amazing team at Coach House Books, in particular Alana Wilcox, Norman Nehmetallah, and Kate Barss.

Jonathan Bartlett for his cover art. This is our third collaboration, and his illustrations make me hope you'll judge my book by its cover.

My partner in life, Aislinn Rose, read various drafts along the way and provided feedback and support for which I'm always grateful.

And finally, to Mitchell Cushman, who first asked me to embark on this voyage and was present every step of the way. The play is better because of his stewardship.

About the Playwright

Nicolas Billon writes for theatre, film, and television. His plays have been performed in multiple languages around the world.

His first play, *The Elephant Song*, was made into a feature film starring Xavier Dolan, Bruce Greenwood, and Catherine Keener, for which he won a Canadian Screen Award and a Writers Guild of Canada Screenwriting Award. His latest, *Butcher*, was produced across Canada and is in development as a feature film with Rhombus Media.

A 2016 graduate of the CFC's Prime Time Television program, Nic recently wrote his first hour of TV drama for CBC's *X Company*.

Nic has won over a dozen awards for his work, including the Governor-General's Award for Drama.

Typeset in Adobe Jenson Pro.

Printed at the Coach House on bpNichol Lane in Toronto, Ontario, on Zephyr Antique Laid paper, which was manufactured, acid-free, in Saint-Jérôme, Quebec, from second-growth forests. This book was printed with vegetable-based ink on a 1973 Heidelberg KORD offset litho press. Its pages were folded on a Baumfolder, gathered by hand, bound on a Sulby Auto-Minabinda and trimmed on a Polar single-knife cutter.

Designed by Norman Nehmetallah
Cover design by Jonathan Bartlett

Coach House Books
80 bpNichol Lane
Toronto ON M5S 3J4
Canada

416 979 2217
800 367 6360

mail@chbooks.com
www.chbooks.com